Evaluating Drug Prevention in the European Union

Papers arising from the 'First European Conference on the Evaluation of Drug Prevention' held in Lisbon, Portugal, 12–14 March 1997

PLANNING GROUP

Margareta Nilson
Gregor Burkhart
Christoph Kröger
Heike Winter

EDITORIAL GROUP

Oswin Baker
Jane Mounteney
Rachel Neaman

E.M.C.D.D.A.
European Monitoring Centre
for Drugs and Drug Addiction

A great deal of additional information on the European Union is available on the Internet. It can be accessed through the Europa server (http://europa.eu.int)

Cataloguing data can be found at the end of this publication

Luxembourg: Office for Official Publications of the European Communities, 1998

ISBN 92-9168-050-8

© European Monitoring Centre for Drugs and Drug Addiction, 1998

Printed in Italy

CONTENTS

ACKNOWLEDGEMENTS

*T*his monograph contains the presentations and deliberations of the 'First European Conference on the Evaluation of Drug Prevention' held in Lisbon from 12–14 March 1997. The volume highlights the work undertaken by the Institut für Therapieforschung (IFT) in Munich – especially by Christoph Kröger and Heike Winter – on behalf of the EMCDDA, as well as the work of others who joined the Centre in investigating the evaluation of drug-prevention initiatives in the European Union: Wim Buismann, Gerhard Christiansen, Mark Morgan, Alice Mostriou, Jorge Negreiros, Teresa Salvador-Llivina, Anne-Marie Sindballe, Zili Sloboda, Alfred Springer, Jürgen Töppich and Alfred Uhl.

Thanks are due to the Conference speakers, workshop leaders and participants whose presentations make up this monograph, the experts who helped peer review the papers and Oswin Baker of the Institute for the Study of Drug Dependence (ISDD) in London who edited them into a coherent whole.

Thanks also go to the staff of the EMCDDA, in particular to Margareta Nilson, Gregor Burkhart, Monika Blum and Sofia Féteira who organised the Conference to the satisfaction of all.

Georges Estievenart
Director
EMCDDA

INTRODUCTION

Preventing drug use is a universal challenge, and identifying which approaches work – and why they work – is a specific challenge for evaluators. In evaluating prevention programmes, not only must the measures of success be established, but a way must also be found to attribute the outcomes either to the programme itself or to some other factor. In addition, it must be possible to compare the effectiveness of different types of intervention in very different settings. This means identifying measures of effectiveness that span the entire prevention field.

None of this is easy, but the potential rewards are enormous. The very process of evaluation can increase communication and ensure that experiences and results are pooled. This sharing of information, in itself, can help in developing future high-quality prevention interventions.

Why a monograph on evaluating drug prevention?

A mere glance at the map of Europe indicates the plethora of philosophies, projects, activities and organisations that exist in the region, all claiming to reduce the demand for drugs. But a closer look at these thousands of interventions reveals that surprisingly few have either been studied or been shown to be demonstrably effective. There are many depressingly familiar reasons for this lack of transparency and scrutiny, in other words for this lack of evaluation.

* *Lack of interest* – prevention activities are often carried out in an *ad hoc* manner, as an immediate response to what is deemed an alarming problem. The aim is usually for something to be 'seen to be done', and there is seldom any further assessment, either of the problem itself or of the intervention's effectiveness.
* *Fear* – many practitioners and programme-planners fear that they will lose funding if evaluation shows that their approach is ineffective. Thus they often opt for a 'soft' evaluation and simple number crunching, rather than undertaking any deeper, more critical analysis.
* *Lack of expertise* – much of the current knowledge about scientific evaluation has been monopolised by a few 'centres of excellence'. These institutions specialise in scientific assessment on a contract-by-contract basis, and receive a large proportion of the funds available for such work. Programme-planners, on the other hand, often do not know how to evaluate an intervention or even how to monitor the work of external evaluators.
* *Cost* – evaluation can be expensive, especially when it is undertaken externally.

Whatever the reasons for it, the lack of rigorous evaluation of drug-prevention activities clearly hinders any improvement in, development or quality control of European programmes. The paucity of evaluation demonstrates that Europe takes a back seat in assessing prevention. In the long term, the lack of commitment to adequate prevention evaluation confirms the scientific community's view that drug prevention is extortionate, uncoordinated and unproved, its survival guaranteed merely because it is 'sexy'.

This was the situation when the European Monitoring Centre for Drugs and Drug Addiction became operational at the end of 1995. One of the major goals of this European Union agency is to improve the image of prevention evaluation in the EU Member States. This was made explicit in the EMCDDA's first demand-reduction Work Programme, which committed the Centre to:

> Improving the quality of prevention activities by assessing the state of the art and examples of good practice of evaluation in the Member States and by promoting the development and improvement of evaluation methodology.

Within this broad framework, the EMCDDA aims to engender a cultural shift in the ideology of prevention. If it is to have any meaningful future, prevention must be scientifically sound, flexible and open to discussion and review. The use of resources – both time and money – must also be scrutinised. The Monitoring Centre's goal is a simple one: to dispel the fear of evaluation by facilitating clear and simple access to its methodology. In addition, the EMCDDA seeks to encourage the view of 'prevention as intervention', where measuring effects and results is routine and where – from the outset – activities are implemented flexibly in accordance with clearly defined objectives.

This monograph marks one of the first milestones of these efforts. It is not the end result, but the beginning of the EMCDDA's project on, and philosophy of, demand reduction.

The EMCDDA programme to evaluate drug prevention

The EMCDDA has initiated a comprehensive programme for evaluating drug prevention. This project involves a number of interdependent elements:

* the organisation of the 'First European Conference on the Evaluation of Drug Prevention', resulting in the publication of this monograph;
* the finalisation of the EMCDDA's *Guidelines for the Evaluation of Drug Prevention* and their worldwide implementation and promotion; and
* the founding of an Evaluation Instrument Bank at the EMCDDA's Lisbon headquarters.

This monograph contains the papers, workshop summaries and a synopsis of the closing roundtable discussion from the 'First European Conference on the Evaluation of Drug Prevention' held on 12–14 March 1997 at the EMCDDA in Lisbon. Some 80 prevention experts and professionals from all over the world participated in the Conference, the first in Europe dedicated exclusively to assessing drug prevention. It was organised to encourage the practice (as well as the theory) of evaluation in Europe, and to promote higher standards, good practice and quality control. It demonstrated that 'prevention works' and that the resources allocated to such activity and its evaluation are well invested.

At the Conference, the first draft of the EMCDDA's *Guidelines for the Evaluation of Drug Prevention* were presented. These *Guidelines* – the final version of which form the companion volume to this monograph – were developed in collaboration with Munich's Institut für Therapieforschung (the German National Focal Point in the REITOX network) and a panel of international experts.

The *Guidelines* offer practical advice on how to ensure optimal quality and good practice in evaluating drug-prevention activities, providing a checklist of all the questions that need to be addressed when evaluating an intervention, together with examples of good practice and a glossary of terms. The *Guidelines* are not only aimed at professionals working in the drug field, but also at scientists, policy-makers and others less directly involved. The publication should enable all to ensure that drug prevention is properly evaluated, and that funding decisions are taken on the basis of the best possible information.

Another important tool of the EMCDDA's evaluation project is the Evaluation Instrument Bank, which follows the structure and philosophy of the *Guidelines*. The Bank is a collection of high-quality, widely used instruments, with a general introduction to implementing and adapting these instruments to specific settings. Each instrument is supported by a commentary, and the Bank is equipped with a search structure for the easy retrieval of instruments for different purposes and contexts. The Bank is to be available on the Internet. A report describing the Bank is currently available at the EMCDDA.

Co-operating partners

The EMCDDA's evaluation project is carried out in partnership with other European institutions and groups active in the drug field. One of its major partners is the Council of Europe's Pompidou Group, which is currently developing a *Handbook for Prevention*. This *Handbook* is intended as a 'pick-and-mix' manual for planning and implementing drug-prevention interventions. This publication and the EMCDDA's *Guidelines* are complementary and cross-reference each other.

The European Commission's COST-A6 programme has also supported several working groups of European researchers in the drug field. In 1997, one of these groups published a Delphi study on evaluating prevention, which serves as an in-depth consensual report on definitions, boundaries, categories and theoretical models of prevention evaluation.[1] It is largely aimed at researchers and scientists and is intended to shed light on the conceptual and terminological 'fog' of evaluation. The terminology used in the *Guidelines* and in the present monograph accords with that agreed in the COST-A6 Delphi study.

---

[1] A Delphi study is a technique for identifying a consensus (or differences) in expert opinion about a given topic and involves at least three waves of questionnaires submitted to an expert panel. A summary feedback from the first wave forms the starting point for the questions in the second wave of the study.

Structure of the monograph

This monograph follows the broad structure of the 'First European Conference on the Evaluation of Drug Prevention'.

Part I on the history of, and background to, evaluating prevention presents a broad overview of the current status of prevention research in Europe and the US, as well as an introduction to the theoretical foundations of evaluation.

Part II deals with the technical and practical aspects of evaluation, highlighting some important examples of research in the field, and providing information on the most commonly encountered methods, instruments, problems and obstacles.

Part III consists of abridged reports of the Conference workshops. These workshops illustrated the role the *Guidelines* could play in the most important and common areas for drug prevention: the mass media; synthetic drug use; community-based initiatives; youth subcultures; schools; and peer groups. The specific features of prevention in these various settings were explained and clarified during the workshops using the participants' own unique experiences.

Part IV summarises the roundtable discussion held at the end of the Conference. A panel of high-ranking experts and policy-makers debated how best to promote evaluation in Europe. In a complex and fascinating exchange, political, societal and scientific points of view were shared. It is this debate – one which is still raging – that will help to clarify the future direction that evaluation in Europe should take.

BACKGROUND
TO EVALUATION

PART I

INTRODUCTION

*T*he first three chapters of this monograph describe the history and current practice of prevention activities and their evaluation.

In Chapter 1, Gerhard Bühringer and Jutta Künzel cover the historical development of prevention and evaluation in Europe, summarising its major results and discussing possible future developments. While clarifying the boundaries of their study, the authors' definitions of relevant terms and related concepts are central to the whole monograph and will be of particular use to readers in later chapters.

Chapter 2 examines the present state of knowledge in the United States, arguably the birthplace of prevention research. Zili Sloboda outlines the main efforts of prevention researchers to create the discipline of prevention science, beginning with a historical summary that describes the evolving theoretical foundation for the field. The author then examines the scientific basis for prevention and assesses the influence of research into the origins of drug misuse. Although it has taken some time to incorporate these theoretical findings into practical prevention, the principles on which effective interventions are based can now be discerned. Sloboda concludes by identifying the gaps that remain in current knowledge about drug prevention and the areas on which future prevention research should concentrate.

Chapter 3 acts as a bridge to Part II by introducing the concept of evaluation and the difficulties this poses for programme-planners. Teresa Salvador-Llivina examines the questions that should be addressed when evaluating prevention interventions. While the need to monitor the effectiveness of prevention is now recognised, the automatic inclusion of evaluation in all prevention programmes is still a long way off. The author discusses the most common difficulties, barriers and problems, touching on issues of planning, funding, implementation analysis and reporting. Salvador-Llivina also details the decision-making process and analyses the benefits and risks of evaluation, while addressing the use to which unexpected outcomes can be put and the need to differentiate between such outcomes and the project's findings.

CHAPTER 1

EVALUATING PREVENTIVE INTERVENTION IN EUROPE

Gerhard Bühringer and Jutta Künzel

Ever since Europe's contemporary drug problem first emerged at the beginning of the 1970s, preventive measures have been taken to reduce the number of drug users. During the 1970s, the political agenda was dominated by treatment efforts, and tended to focus on and allocate most resources to delivering, analysing and improving various forms of care. The limited interest in prevention stemmed from an equally limited understanding of the factors that can influence or encourage drug misuse in individuals, communities and societies.

In the 1980s, prevention became a major area of interest. This was not because the pool of knowledge had expanded, but rather because a growing body of evidence from studies of treatment outcomes had called its effectiveness into doubt. At the same time, epidemiological data demonstrated that the scale of the drug problem had not diminished significantly.

More sophisticated scientific concepts, however, were still required to explain the factors that influence the onset of drug use, and those that can lead to a harmful pattern of drug use or to the cessation of such behaviour. The scientific methodology was only partly available and, in practice, preventive activities rarely included evaluation as an integral tool for monitoring and improving the quality of the work.

Since then, major steps have been taken, both in developing scientifically based theories of prevention, and in implementing them across Europe. Much of this scientific knowledge derives from the United States (see Chapter 2), but there is also a strong tradition of prevention in Europe, especially in the United Kingdom and Scandinavia (Cázares and Beatty, 1994; Leukefeld and Bukoski, 1991; Künzel-Böhmer *et al.*, 1993, 1994).

Drugs, prevention and evaluation: some definitions

Drugs

The term 'drugs' is used in prevention evaluation to describe illicit drugs as identified by international treaties. For practical purposes, no distinction is made here between these drugs (for instance, between 'soft' and 'hard' drugs), even though approaches that classify drugs according to their assumed individual or social risks can be found in nearly all European states.

Psychoactive substances

The term 'psychoactive substances' (or simply 'substances') is used to include other drugs – such as alcohol and tobacco – that affect the central nervous system. It is essential to include such substances in any discussion of prevention – despite social and legal differences – for the following reasons:

- The use of any psychoactive substance enhances the risk of using others (for example, early alcohol and tobacco consumption increases the risk of illicit drug use – Herbst and Kraus, 1995).
- Many factors known to be responsible for the onset of drug use (such as family or peer-group influences) are largely independent of the specific substance used.
- Different substances appear to have biological similarities (for example, cannabis, opiates and alcohol).
- It is more efficient for prevention activities to address all substances, rather than to develop different programmes for different drugs.
- If a prevention intervention is to be credible to the young, it must include licit substances which young people see adults abusing on a daily basis.

For these reasons, most primary drug-prevention programmes do not differentiate between substances. Information on specific drugs is clearly necessary, but providing such information does not play a major role in many preventive activities.

Prevention

The term 'prevention' indicates any activity that seeks to reduce or delay the onset of drug use over a given period. While this definition may seem like common sense, researchers, politicians and practitioners all understand the word differently. Figure 1 illustrates some of the more common interpretations of the term 'prevention'.

Health professionals usually define prevention as any demand-reduction activity intended to modify behaviour and so reduce the desire for drugs. In many cases, this approach is further limited to primary prevention – reducing the wish to *begin* taking drugs. Using the current jargon, this means strengthening 'protective factors' and weakening 'risk factors'. Both groups of factors could relate to an individual's genetic make-up and personality, or to their familial, social and physical environment.

Criminal-justice experts, politicians and probably most of the general public understand prevention to mean supply reduction. The less available a psychoactive substance, the less likely the onset of drug abuse. Examples of prevention to reduce supply include price controls and taxation, limiting access to the substance, public safety and, of course, the threat of punishment. This last approach can range from fines for driving while drunk to total prohibition.

Others stress that prevention is best carried out by raising awareness and promoting 'healthy living' among the population at large. These activities can include public-information campaigns, explicit commitments from politicians to keep the issue at the top of their agendas, and adequate financial support for prevention and teacher training.

Figure 1: Different concepts and intervention strategies in the field of prevention

Demand reduction			
Primary prevention	*Secondary prevention*	*Treatment interventions*	*Tertiary prevention*

1. Protective and risk factors affecting the onset of substance abuse:
- heredity
- family environment (education, modelling)
- peer-group pressures
- social conditions

2. Protective and risk factors affecting heavy substance abuse (early intervention)

3. Protective and risk factors affecting relapse after treatment (relapse prevention):
- external and internal factors
- individual and interactional factors

Supply reduction

1. Price, taxation

2. Limiting access:
- partial or total prohibition
- monopolies
- rationing
- controlling number of outlets
- controlling availability
- regulating drinks according to strength
- regulating hours and days of sale
- protecting children and young people

3. Public safety:
- workplace
- traffic

4. Threat of punishment

Promoting awareness of the problem within the general population

1. Mass-media campaigns

2. Public commitment of politicians

3. Preventive intervention training for relevant others

4. Financial support

These different views of what prevention really means illustrate that the term is a 'movable feast', depending on who is using it. The variety of concepts is further complicated by secondary and tertiary prevention. In these cases, the aim is not to prevent the onset of drug use, but to tackle problem drug use or to prevent an individual who has successfully undergone treatment for drug abuse from reverting to old habits ('relapsing'). Both these concepts overlap with contemporary approaches to treatment (such as early intervention and preventing relapse), which can sometimes blur the boundaries between preventive and treatment strategies.

The concept of prevention has been complicated even further in recent years by the introduction of the term 'harm reduction', a possible variant on secondary prevention. Harm reduction does not target drug abuse *per se*, but rather the onset of a harmful pattern of drug use. In this context, the wish to take drugs is no longer the focus; instead, the aim is to reduce the negative consequences of continuing drug use. Whether such an approach really can be classified as prevention or not is debatable. It can be argued that harm reduction is in fact a pragmatic treatment strategy for those clients unable or unwilling to stop their drug use. At least, the argument goes, they are being encouraged to change their drug-abuse behaviour in a way that reduces the harmful consequences as much as possible.

A final confusion for those wishing to understand prevention is the emergence of the 'civil-rights' argument into the field. There is growing opposition, in Europe at least, to the social need to define certain drugs as 'illicit'. The 'right to take drugs' has become the catchphrase of this approach and, in this light, prevention becomes no longer preventing drug abuse as such, but promoting certain forms of drug use that have few or no harmful consequences. If these harmful consequences are seen predominantly as related to social pressure (punishment, public approbation, and so on) then preventing drug abuse becomes synonymous with abolishing such penalties and – in the extreme – with public support for drug use.

This brief synopsis of the issues involved in defining prevention is not intended to confuse, but to demonstrate the wide degree of understanding of the issue. The variety of approaches to prevention complicates international co-operation and clearly influences how prevention strategies and activities are evaluated.

A detailed history of the various concepts of prevention would far exceed the scope of this chapter. Instead, it will focus on preventive activities as a form of primary prevention within the field of demand reduction. This does not mean that other approaches are ineffective. On the contrary, a recent publication on the social consequences of alcohol abuse clearly demonstrates the effectiveness of supply-reduction activities (see Edwards *et al.*, 1994, 1997).

Evaluation

Evaluation has been defined as 'the systematic application of social research procedures in assessing the conceptualization and design, implementation, and utility of social intervention programmes' (Rossi and Freeman, 1985). Other aspects of evaluation are discussed later in this monograph, but this chapter addresses two major misunderstandings of the concept which mirror those in the field of prevention.

Evaluation is not simply 'something researchers do' each time a new prevention programme needs to be assessed. Instead, it is an integral part of everyday practical work. This does not, of course, mean that every single activity has to be accompanied by a major research project. The level of evaluation in any prevention activity must be adapted to the given situation. The reason why integrating evaluation procedures into everyday practice is so vital is that it guarantees constant feedback on the actual quality of an intervention. This allows any procedure to be adapted in line with changes in the field of prevention and new research findings.

The second misunderstanding comes from the belief that prevention activities can only be evaluated according to their outcome. While this is a major purpose of evaluation, it is not the only one. Evaluation must also include a needs analysis to assess systematically the need for intervention in a particular situation, as well as the design and development of an effective intervention. In addition, evaluation involves a process that analyses the quality of the implementation.

A European history of prevention and evaluation

The relationship between prevention and evaluation is a fundamental one. For example, the effects of different policies on the levels of alcohol-related problems in various countries could only be analysed once adequate statistical methods had been developed and epidemiological data collected (Edwards *et al.*, 1994). The relationship is also a long-standing one (for a more detailed historical analysis, see Völger and Welck, 1982).

While the Bible is among the first written records to tackle drunkenness (with the story of Noah's 'relief' after the flood), the first long descriptions of alcohol use can be found in early Greek literature, which discusses alcohol's positive and negative effects and suggests ways to regulate drinking. Homer, for instance, wrote about Odysseus' behaviour when drunk; Hippocrates gave detailed medical descriptions of the factual and assumed consequences of drunkenness; and Plato was one of the first to draw up drinking regulations according to age (see Preiser, 1982). He declared that up to the age of 18 boys should not drink at all, and up to the age of 30 they could drink, but only in moderation. After 30, however, getting drunk was acceptable! Plato also proposed regulations for prohibition, such as during wars, for all slaves, for drivers, politicians and judges during working hours, for everyone during the day and for men and women when trying to conceive.

In the Middle Ages, the concept that alcohol could be harmful simply did not exist – excessive drinking was fun (Legnaro, 1982). In fact, rituals that included excessive drinking were very important, and daily drinking – including getting drunk at least twice a month – was an essential part of all good medical advice. The literature of the time is full of the positive consequences of drinking, and no notion of preventive activities existed.

With the beginning of the modern age in Europe in the 16th century, the traditionally positive connotations of excessive drinking began to change. The increasing emphasis on self-control and self-determination was applied to drinking behaviour, and drunkenness began to be seen as a sign of weak character. Alcohol lost its dominant position as a major therapeutic agent in the medical literature, and regulation re-emerged after 2,000 years. The first temperance organisations sprang up in Germany in the 1520s and several German parliaments banned 'raising a glass'.

At the same time, the previously uncritical use of opium as a cure-all was also challenged (Schmitz, 1982). The therapeutic use of opium was described for the first time as the *ultima ratio* ('the last resort'), while medical literature was full of detailed descriptions of the drug's negative consequences.

In the 19th century, the Industrial Revolution brought modern techniques to alcohol production. Prices fell and consumption soared, causing another shift in attitudes towards excessive drinking. Mirroring the medical profession's better understanding, alcoholism began to be seen as a disease rather than as a weakness of character.

The modern Temperance Movement took off in the middle of the 19th century in Germany, Scandinavia, the UK, a number of other European countries and the United States. This Movement was encouraged, on the one hand, by doctors wishing to tackle alcohol's effects on health and, on the other, by industrialists wishing to tackle its effects on their businesses (Levine, 1982). The Temperance Movement changed the concept of alcohol-related problems by seeing the substance, not the drinker, as the cause. This left abstinence as the only possible option. Temperance regulated the drinking behaviour of millions, peaking in the 1920s and 1930s with partial or total prohibition in Scandinavia and the US. In addition to this clear 'supply-reduction' approach, large-scale demand-reduction activities emerged for the first time in the latter half of the 19th century. These included mass-media campaigns, pamphlets, paintings, plays and many other social activities and meetings run by local and national 'temperance societies'. In effect, the Temperance Movement was the first large-scale prevention initiative in Europe.

However, this initiative was privately run, and it was only at the turn of the 20th century that the Movement's activities spawned the first comprehensive public approach to alcohol control in Europe. The Scandinavian countries implemented the first alcohol-control policy, with partial and total prohibitions, monopolies, high prices, taxation, rationing and limits on the number of retail outlets and their opening hours. For the first time, a whole society began to understand the relationship between the quantity of alcohol consumed and the level of alcohol-related problems in their country. This was the precondition for what could be defined as the first systematic evaluation of preventive measures. The Scandinavian supply-reduction policy was 'evaluated' in terms of the effect it had on the amount of alcohol consumed, and the number and severity of alcohol-related problems.

At about the same time, preventive techniques began to be applied – at least in theory – to other psychoactive substances. From 1900–20, the volume of medical literature produced on the effects of cocaine and opiates led to the first proposals for concerted supply reduction beyond the general warning given by doctors to their patients. This emphasis on measures to reduce supply dominated the first half of the 20th century.

In the 1950s, the early seeds of preventive activity in the field of demand reduction were sown. The need for various demand-reduction activities was formally discussed at conferences in 1953 and 1959, and although there was almost no scientific knowledge base, personal experience and intuition produced some very modern thinking, for example that:

- attitudes should be changed and accurate information disseminated;
- prevention should not just be drug-specific, but should be related to the whole person;
- observing parents has a major influence on children's use of alcohol, whether positive or negative; and
- a positive family environment is important for avoiding alcohol-related problems (Deutsche Hauptstelle gegen die Suchtgefahren, 1954, 1961).

In the early 1970s, Bejerot attempted to evaluate Sweden's supply-reduction measures for illicit drugs (Bejerot, 1975). He concluded that liberal laws increase – and repressive laws decrease – drug use and drug-related problems. This debate is still as powerful today as it was then, but as the methodology of time-series analysis was relatively unsophisticated then, it can now be argued that Bejerot's methodological analysis does not support his conclusions.

Despite Bejerot's findings, there was a move away from supply reduction to demand reduction in the 1970s, a shift that gained more and more authority as preventive concepts and programmes became accepted in modern research. Three phases can be distinguished in the decades since then (Künzel-Böhmer et al., 1993):

- *Information dissemination*, based on moral principles, factual knowledge and fear arousal.
- *Value clarification*, based on concepts of self-worth and developing positive alternatives to drug use.
- *Risk factors and protective factors*, based on increasingly strong empirical research.

With hindsight, and given the modern emphasis on scientific analysis, it is hardly surprising that the concept of evaluation began to increase in importance. In 1979, the United Nations published a report on measures to reduce the demand for illicit drugs (United Nations, 1979). This report summarised the major research findings of the time, and the clear message was that evaluating prevention activities would be pivotal in future. The report highlighted not only the need for evaluation, but also the need for a balance of supply- and demand-reduction activities in prevention initiatives; the need to educate the public about alternatives to drug use; programmes to cope with adolescent problems; and the need to incorporate drug-abuse prevention into health education.

The next step was the UN Expert Group on Drug Abuse Reduction, which met in Vienna in 1983 (Expert Group on Drug Abuse Reduction, 1983). This Group also called for a balance of supply- and demand-reduction measures, and for the promotion of 'positive alternatives to drug use'. For the first time, it urged that licit substances be included in prevention programmes, but the Group also demanded a critical evaluation of fear-based information activities and a positive evaluation of long-term school, parental and community programmes. For this to be achievable, the Expert Group recommended training educational staff in schools and workplaces and called for simple, 'off-the-shelf' evaluation techniques based on an adaptive learning system that would allow preventive activities to be continually analysed and improved.

Alongside these conceptual and regulatory developments, the basic information needed to improve not only prevention, but also its evaluation, was collected and analysed much more systematically and on a larger scale. By the early 1980s, the quantity and quality of epidemiological surveys in Europe, and of prevention research and evaluation technology in the United States, was such that a number of new techniques and programmes could be developed. Chief among these were:

- the concept of 'social inoculation' to resist drug offers (Evans, 1976);
- the Life-Skills Training programme (Botvin and Wills, 1985);
- the evaluation of national mass-media campaigns in Germany, Sweden and the UK (for example, Bühringer *et al.*, 1994); and
- the evaluation of modern school-based programmes in Greece, the Netherlands and Scandinavia (for example, Mostriou *et al.*, 1995).

By the mid-1980s, all the necessary components for modern preventive concepts and interventions were in place. First, epidemiological information about the size and structure of the problem was widely available. Second, the theoretical concepts of risk and the factors that could protect against the onset and development of substance abuse had been developed. Finally, the prevention programmes themselves that used both this information and theory were well under way, and the first body of research to evaluate the effectiveness of these approaches was in the public domain.

Over the last 50 years, the dominant prevention approach has shifted from supply reduction to demand reduction, and, in the last few years, slightly back again. This final move seems to be based on an understanding that modern prevention has to use all the tools available, and that more research is needed to determine the proper balance of these approaches.

The current state of evaluation

It is somewhat artificial to define when modern, large-scale prevention activities in Europe first began, but 1986 is as good a starting point as any. In 1986, the World Health Organisation (WHO) Regional Office for Europe launched the 'Healthy City Network'. Twenty European cities joined together in a common effort to reduce substance abuse and, for the first time in a large-scale programme, evaluation played an integral role (WHO, 1994).

In 1990, the European Community – building on the WHO's work – increased its prevention efforts with another large-scale programme. The European Drug Prevention Weeks of 1992 and 1994 were part of this effort, and three European Action Plans against drugs, alcohol and tobacco were launched, all of which explicitly included evaluation.

The high levels of acceptance that evaluation now inspired were graphically demonstrated in a 1992 survey of over 1,100 European prevention projects. The survey found that 54% of these projects included some type of evaluation, even though the quality varied among them (Centro de Estudios sobre Promoción de la Salud, 1992). Two years later, the Council of Europe's Pompidou Group launched a three-year work programme which specifically covered prevention evaluation.

At the same time, the COST-A6 prevention working group concentrated on the 'evaluation of primary prevention'. The group held workshops (on topics as varied as evaluating drug education in schools and the sociocultural aspects of primary prevention) and produced a Delphi study on the format and content of primary prevention evaluation.

In 1996, on behalf of the EMCDDA, the Institut für Therapieforschung, Munich, conducted a survey of European prevention programmes that had already been evaluated. This survey informed the development of the Monitoring Centre's *Guidelines for the Evaluation of Drug Prevention*, a companion to this volume. The same year, the EMCDDA published its 1995 *Annual Report on the State of the Drugs Problem in the European Union* (EMCDDA, 1996), of which the major conclusions relating to prevention were:

- Prevention today is generally understood to be primary prevention within the general strategy of demand reduction, rather than in the field of supply reduction.
- Prevention interventions exist all over Europe, but are predominantly school-based.
- Prevention interventions are based more and more regularly on modern research-based knowledge.
- Prevention interventions are more regularly evaluated.

The above brief outline has demonstrated that in the last ten years, prevention has shifted from being a limited research tool to being implemented under the aegis of European public bodies. This implementation has helped to integrate prevention and evaluation, so that the result – prevention evaluation – is now a normal and necessary part of any co-ordinated action against drug abuse.

Examples of evaluated projects

The following examples of prevention programmes illustrate the types of intervention currently being evaluated in Europe (Bundeszentrale für gesundheitliche Aufklärung, 1995). The list is not exhaustive, but demonstrates the wide variety of approaches to evaluating prevention interventions.

Development of secondary-school drug-educational material (Austria)

In 1991, this programme developed educational materials for teachers to use in secondary schools within the general curriculum. The materials contained both drug-specific and non-specific components. The main theoretical framework was that poor life skills can precipitate drug problems. The non-specific components, therefore, aimed to promote such skills and self-awareness in schoolchildren. The project was evaluated using questionnaires completed by both pupils and teachers six months after the programme began. In general, both groups assessed the materials positively. At the end of the project, one-third of the 665 pupils had a more critical view of their own consumption behaviour.

Evaluating the 'Mia's diary' school programme (Denmark, Finland, Norway, Sweden)

'Mia's diary' is a school-based prevention programme for pupils aged 13–15 (Nersnaes, 1995), and is used in all the Nordic countries except Iceland. The programme, presented in the form of a diary written by Mia, a 15-year-old, takes as its theoretical basis Botvin's Life-Skills Training (see Chapter 2). The project's main aim is to strengthen social skills, thus enabling children actively to resist pressure to take drugs. The programme was evaluated in 1994, with data collected from about 1,500 schoolchildren in Denmark, Finland, Norway and Sweden (Nersnaes, 1995). The evaluation was carried out using questionnaires completed by a selected group of classes before and after they had finished the programme. The evaluation found that the project had increased the level of knowledge about substance abuse, but had not had any significant impact on attitudes. The lack of attitudinal change was partly explained by insufficient evaluation methods.

The 'ALF' school prevention programme (Germany)

ALF is a life-skills training programme for schoolchildren aged 10–14. It was conducted by trained teachers in Bavarian schools, and – for evaluative purposes – compared two versions of the curriculum (with and without specific information about psychotropic substances). After the first 12 sessions, the evaluation results for the group that had received specific information about tobacco and alcohol were very positive. The number of smokers had not increased, whereas the number of smokers in the control group had nearly doubled.

School-based health-education programme (Greece)

In the late 1980s, a health-education programme to prevent drug abuse was piloted in two secondary schools (see, for example, Mostriou *et al.*, 1995). Both drug-specific and non-specific elements were included in the programme, with the latter aimed at developing life skills. The materials used had been translated from Swedish and English and then adapted to the Greek environment, and the programme was carried out by specially trained teachers. Students were encouraged to participate in community activities, while community leaders were encouraged to take part in activities aimed at informing and mobilising the general public on health issues. Evaluation data were collected from students, community leaders and officials using questionnaires and personal interviews. The results were positive, especially those related to student attitudes towards drug use, which shifted in the desired direction.

Drug prevention in schools (Ireland)

From 1992–94, the Substance Abuse Prevention Project was carried out as a pilot scheme in eight secondary schools in Ireland (Morrow, 1995). During the project, classroom materials were developed and piloted, teachers implementing the programme trained and supported, and interventions started at an organisational level to maximise school support for the programme's goals. The programme contained drug-specific and non-specific elements, and was mainly aimed at developing and encouraging children's identity, self-esteem, communication and decision-making skills. During the trial phase, the project was evaluated. The methods and results included:

* teacher feedback on the materials, which was incorporated before the final printing;
* evaluation of teacher training, which reported a high level of satisfaction;
* the reactions of teachers and students, which were very positive on the content of the programme itself, the teaching and the class atmosphere;
* interviews with head teachers and staff members, which again were very positive; and
* a comparative study (pilot schools versus control schools), which found that children at the pilot schools had a more negative attitude towards drugs, greater knowledge about the consequences of drug use and better developed life skills than those at the control schools.

Prevention of alcohol and tobacco use in elementary schools (the Netherlands)

Based on the assumption that 12 is the best age for preventive education, a programme for primary schools was established in 1985 (Spruyt, 1995). Its main objectives were to enable children to resist peer pressure and advertising messages, and to develop a reasonable attitude towards the use of alcohol and tobacco. The programme was evaluated between 1985 and 1988. An experimental and a control group completed questionnaires on four separate occasions (before the programme began, and six, 12 and 36 months after it ended). Results from the six- and 12-month follow-ups were encouraging. Knowledge about the risks of smoking and drinking were good, and delayed the onset of these behaviours. Unfortunately, the effects appeared to decrease after three years, indicating that continuing the programme is a very important element.

Primary drug-prevention programme (Portugal)

In 1989, a community drug-prevention project was set up for young people aged 12–19 in two communities in Portugal. The basis for the project was an epidemiological study of the psychosocial aspects of drug use, the general interests and drug consumption of the target group (Correia da Silva, 1995). Based on the results of this survey, an intervention model was developed that included activities in young people's groups as well as community interventions. The model aims to promote a healthy lifestyle, the active participation of young people in the community, knowledge about jobs and the world of work, and to reduce risky behaviour. The activities were evaluated by questionnaires and individual interviews with the participants and their parents, although this evaluation was geared more towards the project's 'effects' than its 'efficiency'.

Conclusions

Taking into account modern drug-prevention theories, current knowledge of the initiation and development of substance use and the actual state of evaluation, the following conclusions can be drawn.

A comprehensive prevention approach requires both supply- and demand-reduction measures. Research – especially into alcohol issues, where policy differences between countries make comparative evaluation easier – has shown that demand-reduction measures must be supplemented by supply-reduction measures (Edwards *et al.*, 1994). While more research is undoubtedly needed to 'weight' demand and supply measures correctly, the fact itself can no longer be questioned.

Modern demand-reduction activities in primary prevention are based on a probabilistic theory of how harmful use develops, and explain it through 'protective' and 'risk' factors. It is obvious that no single factor is responsible for the development of drug abuse. Genetic, psychological and environmental conditions all play a role in this process, both as potential risk and protective factors. This 'biopsychosocial' concept means that a broad range of risk factors must be taken into account, and also that a variety of protective factors must be supported. As with demand and supply reduction, the relative weight of risk and protective factors is largely unknown, and so for practical purposes both types of factor should be taken into account.

Major risk factors include family education and parenting styles (such as lack of support in identifying problems and a failure to build self-confidence), while substance use in the family ('copycat' behaviour), peer pressure and the general availability of drugs must also be monitored. This points towards the need for more activities in the family, especially in early childhood, and indicates that prevention measures should start early – among six-to-ten-year-olds – before peer-group influence usurps family influence.

Major protective factors include promoting certain life skills and drug-specific resistance training. As with treatment approaches, prevention evaluation is still in its infancy and few long-term results of such interventions are available. But those programmes that have been evaluated clearly support the promotion of certain life skills, such as self-confidence, problem-solving, communication skills, stress management and drug-specific resistance training (for example, learning how to refuse drugs).

Most current prevention is either carried out in schools or via public-information campaigns, but comprehensive community-based approaches (making use of the family, youth centres, local businesses, the police, and so on) have also been shown to improve the outcome. In fact, focusing on families (particularly those with young children) would perhaps be more beneficial, as well as targeting the workplace and the health system. On the other hand, 'one-off' time-limited prevention activities are of little value.

The appropriateness of a particular prevention activity is also crucial. Public-information campaigns, for example, cannot change harmful use (they may even increase it) and should not be used for this purpose. Drug users, therefore, should not be the target group for a public-information campaign. Such campaigns can, however, promote public awareness and support for financing prevention activities. They can, in turn, provide support for specific groups, such as parents and youth-club leaders.

In other words, preventive measures should start early, take a long-term approach and avoid flashy spectacle. But just as important is the *basis* for any intervention. Prevention is only effective with actual experimental research and continual evaluation. Without research, prevention has no foundation; but without evaluation, it has no future. Continuing evaluation is essential for assessing the initial situation ('needs analysis'), for planning and carrying out prevention activities adequately and to a high standard ('process evaluation'), and for adapting the approach depending on the results ('outcome evaluation').

Future perspectives

In general, it appears that in the field of drug prevention and its evaluation much more is known in theory than is implemented in practice. The first and overriding future need must therefore be to make proper use of research findings. This means that scientific advances must be communicated to practitioners in a way that they understand and can use in their daily work. Other vital demands are:

- Both prevention and evaluation must be integral to the job descriptions of local and regional authorities and practitioners in the health and social-care field. This is necessary not only for those who specialise in prevention, but also for those with a broad range of health and social-care responsibilities.
- As with environmental protection, it is absolutely vital that politicians and the media publicly support drug-prevention activities and the need for continuing evaluation.

- More research is needed into the balance between supply and demand reduction in prevention. Until recently, this discussion has been predominantly influenced by beliefs rather than by scientific knowledge. While accepting the place for values, the debate is sterile without research into the balance between the two approaches.
- More research is needed into early family intervention, peer-group intervention and intervention in the workplace. While there is some knowledge of risk and protective factors, the major role of family education/parenting styles and modelling behaviour, as well as peer-group influence, is neither reflected in the level of research nor in the level of practical actions.

Ultimately, however, it must be acknowledged that the progress made in the last decade is astonishing. After many years of imperceptible change and one-off, unsupported prevention activities, public and scientific awareness of large-scale research projects and prevention intervention in Europe since 1985 has soared. It is now abundantly clear that the concept of prevention will play an increasingly important role in European, national and local health and social politics.

References

Bejerot, N. (1975) *Drug Abuse and Drug Policy. An Epidemiological and Methodological Study of Intravenous Drug Abuse in the Stockholm Police Arrest Population 1965–1970 in Relation to Changes in Drug Policy,* Copenhagen: Munksgaard.

Botvin, G., and Wills, T. (1985) *Personal and Social Skills Training: Cognitive-behavioral Approaches to Substance Abuse Prevention,* Rockville, MD: National Institute on Drug Abuse (NIDA).

Bühringer, G., *et al.* (1994) *Evaluation der Kampagne 'Keine Macht den Drogen'. IFT-Berichte Bd. 77,* Munich: Institut für Therapieforschung (IFT).

Bundeszentrale für gesundheitliche Aufklärung (BzgA) (Ed.) (1995) *Die Seminare Sammlung der Referate. Europäische Woche der Suchtprävention 15.–22. Oktober 1994,* Cologne: BzgA.

Cázares, A., and Beatty, L. (Eds) (1994) *Scientific Methods for Prevention Intervention Research,* Rockville, MD: NIDA.

Centro de Estudios sobre la Promoción de la Salud (Ed.) (1992) *EPAS: European Prevention Assessment System 1992. Building up European Cooperation in Drug Abuse Prevention,* Lisbon: European Monitoring Centre for Drugs and Drug Addiction (EMCDDA).

Correia da Silva, M. L. (1995) 'Reflection on a practical experience – a professional point of view on a primary prevention programme of drug abuse in youngsters', in BzgA (Ed.).

Deutsche Hauptstelle gegen die Suchtgefahren (Ed.) (1954) *Schützt unsere Jugend! 4. Kongreß für alkohol- und tabakfreie Jugenderziehung vom 12. bis 15. Oktober 1953 in Bielefeld,* Hamburg: Neuland.

Deutsche Hauptstelle gegen die Suchtgefahren (Ed.) (1961) *Für die Jugend – mit der Jugend. Bericht über den 5. Kongreß für alkohol- und tabakfreie Jugenderziehung vom 21. bis 23. Oktober 1959 in Kassel,* Hamburg: Neuland.

Edwards, G., *et al.* (1994) *Alcohol Policy and the Public Good,* Oxford: Oxford University Press.

Edwards, G., *et al.* (1997) *Alkoholkonsum und Gemeinwohl Strategien zur Reduzierung des schädlichen Gebrauchs in der Bevölkerung,* Stuttgart: Ferdinand Enke Verlag.

European Monitoring Centre for Drugs and Drug Addiction (Ed.) (1996) *1995 Annual Report on the State of the Drugs Problem in the European Union,* Lisbon: EMCDDA.

Evans, R. (1976) 'Smoking in children: Developing a social psychological strategy of deterrence', *Preventive Medicine,* 5(1),122–127.

Expert Group on Drug Abuse Reduction (1983) 'Report of the Expert Group on Drug Abuse Reduction', *Bulletin on Narcotics,* 35(3), 317.

Herbst, K., and Kraus, L. (1995) 'Die "Verschiebung" des Einstiegsalters bei Heroinkonsumenten – Eine Studie zur Epidemiologie des Drogenkonsums', *Zeitschrift für Klinische Psychologie,* 24(2), 90–97.

Künzel-Böhmer, J., *et al.* (1993) *Expertise zur Primärprävention des Substanzmißbrauchs,* Baden-Baden: Nomos.

Künzel-Böhmer, J., *et al.* (1994) *Expert Report on Primary Prevention of Substance Abuse,* Munich: IFT.

Legnaro, A. (1982) 'Alkoholkonsum und Verhaltenskontrolle – Bedeutungswandel zwischen Mittelalter und Neuzeit in Europa', in Völger, G., and Welck, K. (Eds) (1982) *Rausch und Realität 1. Drogen im Kulturvergleich,* Reinbek beim Hamburg: Rowohlt.

Leukefeld, C., and Bukoski, W. (Eds) (1991) *Drug Abuse Prevention Intervention Research: Methodological Issues,* Rockville, MD: NIDA.

Levine, H. (1982) 'Die Entdeckung der Sucht Wandel der Vorstellung über Trunkenheit in Nordamerika', in Völger, G., and Welck, K. (Eds) (1982) *Rausch und Realität 1. Drogen im Kulturvergleich,* Reinbek beim Hamburg: Rowohlt.

Morrow, R. (1995) 'Drug prevention in schools', in BzgA (Ed.).

Mostriou, A., *et al.* (1995) 'Evaluation of the health education pilot program for the prevention of drug abuse in two secondary schools', unpublished manuscript.

Nersnaes, L. (1995) *Livet, Kärleken och Alkoholen. Evaluering av upplysningsprogrammet – "Mias dagbok",* NAD Publication 30, Helsinki: Nordic Council for Alcohol and Drug Research.

Preiser, G. (1982) 'Wein im Urteil der griechischen Antike', in Völger, G., and Welck, K. (Eds) (1982) *Rausch und Realität 2. Drogen im Kulturvergleich,* Reinbek beim Hamburg: Rowohlt.

Rossi, P., and Freeman, H. (1985) *Evaluation. A Systematic Approach,* Beverly Hills, CA: Sage.

Schmitz, R. (1982) 'Opium als Heilmittel', in Völger, G., and Welck, K. (Eds) (1982) *Rausch und Realität 2. Drogen im Kulturvergleich,* Reinbek beim Hamburg: Rowohlt.

Spruyt, R. (1995) 'Prevention of alcohol and tobacco in elementary schools: evaluation results', in BzgA (Ed.).

United Nations (Ed.) (1979) *Study on Measures to Reduce Illicit Demand for Drugs. Preliminary Report of a Working Group of Experts,* New York: United Nations.

Völger, G., and Welck, K. (Eds) (1982) *Rausch und Realität 1, 2, 3. Drogen im Kulturvergleich,* Reinbek beim Hamburg: Rowohlt.

WHO (1994) *Multi-City Action Plan on Drugs,* Copenhagen: WHO Regional Office for Europe.

STATE OF THE ART
OF PREVENTION RESEARCH
IN THE UNITED STATES

Zili Sloboda

In the United States, research into preventing drug abuse has evolved, slowly and painfully, into a science. This evolution required the development not only of measurement instruments, but also of evaluation methodologies – both experimental and non-experimental – and the creation of a detailed epidemiological knowledge base. Furthermore, sound behavioural-change theory and a clear understanding of the pharmacological effects of drugs were vital if prevention researchers were to develop theories and effective strategies to tackle drug abuse.

At the outset, it is important to differentiate 'research' from 'evaluation' from 'science'. Each term addresses different questions and issues. *Research* is the process used to discover a set of principles or laws that have been replicated through systematic approaches. *Evaluation* is a research approach that specifically determines the level of effectiveness of an intervention strategy. In the United States, the attempt to integrate both research and evaluation in order to specify principles of prevention established prevention *science*. This process relied on a set of empirically based theories, accepted terminology, standardised measurements, and agreed research designs and data-analysis methodologies.

In 1989, in a bid to develop the field into a science, the National Institute on Drug Abuse (NIDA), based in Rockville, Maryland, held a succession of meetings to solicit some level of agreement on theory, design, measurement and analytical approaches. The outcomes of these meetings are documented in a series of monographs and papers, and laid the foundations of prevention science. A guide for prevention planners and practitioners setting out the principles of successful prevention intervention was also produced, and the Society for Prevention Research was established in 1991.

This chapter outlines the often overlooked battle fought by the many unsung prevention researchers over three decades. It documents their struggles and their victories, and the history of their work highlights the importance not only of good research approaches, but also of integrating and translating theory into effective interventions.

The history of prevention research in the United States

In a recent paper (Botvin, forthcoming) the author points out:

> The goal of identifying effective prevention approaches has been illusive. While many approaches have increased knowledge of the adverse consequences of using drugs and some have increased anti-drug attitudes, very few programs have demonstrated an impact on drug use behavior.

The last 50 years of US research into drug-prevention illustrate Botvin's point very clearly. The post-war development of health-related behaviour theory was heavily influenced by scare tactics used by the United States Army during the Second World War to discourage negative – and reinforce positive – health behaviour among the troops. It was this theoretical base, in conjunction with empirical data and informed observations, that shaped the drug-abuse prevention approaches of the 1950s and 1960s. Since then, US prevention research has progressed rapidly from strategies emphasising information dissemination and affective education, to social influence and skills building.

Information-dissemination programmes were based on the presumption that individuals are capable of rational decision-making. The belief was that once children knew the negative consequences of drug use, they would choose not to use drugs. Fear-arousal techniques were sometimes used to emphasise the dangers more forcefully.

However, evaluations of such programmes have failed to demonstrate any positive effects on behaviour, although they have shown that knowledge of the harmful aspects of drugs increased, as, in some cases, did a negative attitude towards drug use (Swisher and Hoffman, 1975; Dorn and Thompson, 1976; Schaps et al., 1981).

Early research also suggested that the onset of drug use was associated with a degree of confusion about it. 'Affective-education' programmes were therefore developed, focusing on issues such as 'values clarification', 'self-understanding' and effective communication. Again, evaluations failed to demonstrate the effectiveness of such programmes against drug use, although, once more, many did have an impact on associative factors, such as feelings of self-worth (Kearney and Hines, 1980; Kim, 1988).

The theoretical and scientific basis for prevention

In the late 1970s, largely supported by the NIDA, a national research programme was initiated. This consisted of prospective studies of children and adolescents to determine the origins of, and routes to, drug abuse. In addition, the NIDA designed a system to monitor household and high-school surveys to give an informed estimate of the nature and extent of substance misuse. The results of these and other studies gave researchers a fresh perspective on the origins of drug abuse, and a new era in which to advance prevention research began.

Perhaps one of the most important outcomes of the research at that time was the by-now almost commonplace ability to pinpoint the 'age of initiation' into drug use. For example, the results of long-term epidemiological studies suggest that most drug users begin between the ages of 12 and 17.

The onset of tobacco and alcohol use, both of which have been associated with the use of cannabis and other drugs, generally occurs earlier, largely due to the easy availability and social acceptance of these substances. The 'sequence' of use from tobacco and alcohol to cannabis and then on to other drugs has been a consistent finding in almost all longitudinal studies of young people (Kandel *et al.*, 1992; Newcomb and Bentler, 1986). But 'sequencing' does not imply 'inevitability' – that because someone smokes cigarettes or drinks alcohol they will automatically use cannabis or other drugs. Rather, it shows that among tobacco and alcohol users, the risk of progressing to cannabis is much higher (an estimated 65 times) than if an individual had never smoked or drunk. Likewise, the risk of graduating to cocaine is higher (an estimated 104 times) for those who have taken cannabis than for those who have not (NIDA, 1996).

No research has been able to explain the mechanisms underlying these connections. But what these findings suggest is that interventions should focus on children at an early age and must attempt to prevent or delay the onset of tobacco and alcohol use. They also suggest that prevention interventions should be appropriately designed for the developmental stage of the specific age group.

Patterns of use

As well as identifying precisely the age of initiation, research has also uncovered patterns of use. Trend analyses of school-age drug use – such as the national survey of eighth, tenth and twelfth graders (the 'Monitoring the Future' study) – have shown two clear patterns in the prevalence of drug use over time.[1] First, they demonstrate that the use of illicit substances increases with age, with the highest levels of use among the twelfth graders. Second, the trend analyses show that cannabis use, which had been declining during the 1980s, began to rise in 1992 across all three age groups, with continued increases each year, particularly among the younger students (Johnston *et al.*, 1996). The challenge facing the prevention practitioner is to slow this upward trajectory, and the challenge facing the epidemiologist is to understand why these new increases are occurring.

Several hypotheses have been posited, but studies addressing this issue are still too preliminary to be conclusive. It is known, however, that these trends have been preceded by changes in the students' perceptions of the harmful effects of cannabis and

[1] The 'Monitoring the Future' study, supported by a grant from the NIDA since 1974, is conducted by the Institute for Survey Research of the University of Michigan. Until 1991, the study was administered annually in the classroom among approximately 17,000 seniors attending a national probability sample of both public and high schools, beginning with the class of 1975. In 1991, the survey was expanded to similar numbers of eighth- and tenth-grade students.

its social acceptability. Earlier, increased negative perceptions had likewise been associated with decreases in use (Bachman *et al.*, 1990 and 1988). This suggests that, in order to influence their attitudes, prevention programmes must seek to provide young people with accurate information about the health risks and consequences of drug use.

Risk and protective factors

Furthermore, studies that track young people over time clearly show that the process of initiating or continuing drug use is highly complex, involving many factors. These range from genetics, biology, personality and psychology to the family, school experiences, peer pressure and environmental influences (Hawkins *et al.*, 1992; Pandina, forthcoming). The strongest influences on initial drug use, however, are interpersonal relationships – the family and peer groups.

Much information is available on 'family process' and the initiation of drug-using behaviour. These factors include the quality of the parent–child relationship and of parent–child attachment; the quality of parenting; the consistent enforcement of rules and boundaries; the establishment of a supportive environment; the clarification of norms against drug use; and family identification and bonding (McCord and McCord, 1959; Jessor and Jessor, 1977; Hirschi, 1969; Brook *et al.*, 1990; Cohen *et al.*, 1990; Cadoret *et al.*, 1986; Shedler and Block, 1990; Demarsh and Kumpfer, 1986; Kaplan, 1985; Kandel *et al.*, 1978; Pandina and Johnson, 1989; Patterson *et al.*, 1992).

Interventions that aim to improve parenting practices have actually reduced the onset of drug use, even when these interventions target adolescents (Bry and Canby, 1986; Friedman, 1989; Lewis *et al.*, 1990; Schmidt *et al.*, 1996). Interventions aimed at younger children have not followed the subjects for long enough to observe any impact on drug use (Webster-Stratton, 1984 and 1990), although significant improvements in parent–child relationships and school behaviour have already been observed. In fact, for the more vulnerable populations, it has been found that without including the family in the intervention, family functioning can rapidly deteriorate, while 'risk' can increase not only for the individual, but also for other family members (Szapocznik and Kurtines, 1989; Dishion and Andrews, 1995; Dishion *et al.*, 1996).

In addition, epidemiological studies have found that peers can make drugs accessible and encourage and reinforce drug use, while 'peer pressure' or 'modelling behaviour' is also closely allied to the initiation and continuation of drug use. Further links have been found between drug use and other social factors, such as poor school performance, failure to internalise educational norms and lack of identification with school rules. A number of factors associated with the individual have also been identified. These include low self-esteem, poor self-control and inadequate social coping skills. Other factors identified by the research are tolerance of deviant attitudes, sensation seeking, stressful life events, depression and anxiety.

In addition, it has been found that the more of these an individual experiences, the greater the likelihood of drug use or abuse. This all suggests that prevention interventions should address 'risk', while also aiming to enhance 'protective' factors.

Developmental stages

People are most vulnerable when in transition from one developmental stage to another, and thus prevention should occur throughout the life cycle, particularly during stressful periods of change. One example is the change children undergo when moving from elementary school to middle school or junior high, when they often face social challenges and pressures, such as learning to get on with a wider group of peers. It is at this stage, early adolescence, that children are likely to encounter drug use for the first time. Later on, when they enter high school and face further social, psychological and educational hurdles, they will again be exposed to 'risk' situations. Even when young adults go to college, get married or enter the workforce, they face risks in their 'new' adult environment. Therefore, as risks are present at every transition from infancy to young adulthood, prevention-planners need to develop programmes that provide the necessary support at each developmental stage.

Laboratory research

Basic laboratory research is also critical to the design of prevention interventions, not only because it stretches the bounds of knowledge, but also because it can act as a credible educational tool or resource to demonstrate the pharmacological and physiological effects of drugs to youngsters.

For example, the new brain-imaging technologies, such as magnetic resonance imaging (MRI) and computerised axial tomography (CAT) scans, allow the living human brain to be viewed. This has implications for drug research, because these techniques can identify the basic brain mechanisms involved in addiction and the specific areas in the brain where these effects occur (Volkow *et al.*, 1991; Childress *et al.*, 1995; Altman, 1996). Craving and other physiological processes that are significantly altered in the dependent state have also now been understood. Such information can be effective in prevention programmes by demonstrating the negative impact of drugs.

Applying research findings to effective prevention interventions

Evans and his colleagues (Evans, 1976; Evans *et al.*, 1978) were among the first to make use of such findings and theories in developing a novel prevention approach – social inoculation. This approach was used to counter pro-smoking messages from peers, family and the media by arming children with the skills to identify the source of the pressure and to resist it. The programme also sought to demonstrate that smoking was not a normative behaviour. This was the first time that a theoretical basis had been applied to the use of illicit drugs. Over the next two decades, variations on the social-inoculation model were widely tested, and the combination of training in drug-resistance skills and decision-making, as well as correcting misperceptions of the normative nature of drug abuse, has been demonstrated time and again to be effective in preventing drug use (Hansen and Graham, 1991; Botvin *et al.*, 1995; Pentz *et al.*, 1989).

Life-Skills Training

An excellent recent example of a successful programme to have emerged from this perspective is Life-Skills Training (LST), developed by Gilbert Botvin, which incorporates both social-learning theory (Bandura, 1977) and problem-behaviour theory (Jessor and Jessor, 1977). In this context, drug abuse is viewed as learned and functional behaviour, encouraged by social influences. Life-Skills Training does what it says – it combines training in basic interpersonal skills with information about the risks and prevalence of drug abuse, all held together by training in the skills and knowledge to resist social pressure.

In a recent study of 56 high schools in New York State, LST sessions were given to seventh graders (with an average age of 13), with booster sessions in both eighth and ninth grade. By the end of the twelfth grade, students who had received the full programme reported significantly reduced levels of tobacco, alcohol and cannabis use than those who did not receive the training (Botvin, forthcoming).

Adolescent Transitions Program

Other programmes have focused on indirect factors that have been found to decrease the potential for drug use. These protective factors include good performance at school and strong bonds with social institutions, such as the family, school and church. Given the family's key role and function in any society, and its central position in theories of drug-use initiation, it is hardly surprising that the family is the target and mechanism for many drug-abuse prevention interventions.

The school-based Adolescent Transitions Program, developed by Thomas Dishion, specifically focuses on parenting practices. Targeting the families of young adolescents in middle and junior high school, it sets up a 'Family Resource Room' equipped with a video and other materials designed to help parents identify risk factors. The programme aims to teach effective family-management skills, including positive reinforcement, monitoring, limit-setting and relationship-building. It also offers the 'Family Check-Up', a service that allows family members to assess any problems they may be having. They can then seek professional support, either in a Parent Focus or Teen Focus curriculum. Studies of this and other similar parent-focused interventions have indicated their effectiveness for high-risk young people, with repeated booster sessions throughout the period of risk.

Seattle's Social-Development Project

Other researchers have focused on the risk factors found in the school setting. Academic failure, antisocial behaviour, awkwardness and lack of confidence have all been targeted by effective interventions. One such pilot programme is designed to promote social bonding through a comprehensive family, school and peer-focused prevention programme (Hawkins *et al.*, 1992). Using instructional methods, students are taught about effective learning, co-operation with their peers and positive attitudes towards school. They are also taught peer-refusal skills to help them resist social pressure to use drugs. At the same time, parents are trained to increase their children's involvement in the family and teach them to withstand peer pressure.

Preliminary results for this programme (preliminary, because the children in the study are only now entering adolescence) reveal positive outcomes in five areas:

* a reduction in antisocial behaviour;
* an improvement in academic skills;
* increased commitment to school;
* reduced levels of alienation and poor bonding; and
* reduced misbehaviour at school.

In addition, fewer incidents of drug-taking on school premises have been reported (O'Donnell *et al.*, 1995).

The model for this type of integrated, comprehensive approach to preventing drug abuse is the programme of community-based interventions designed to combat heart disease in the United States (Farquhar *et al.*, 1990). This approach was founded in turn on observations by Sechrest (1985) and others (Cassel, 1976) that interventions to change people's lifestyle and behaviour had to move from the clinic out into the community. Despite some initially mixed results, recent findings show that for those most at risk of cardiovascular illness and death, the comprehensive nature of the programme – using a wide range of media and settings – supported change (Winkleby *et al.*, 1994).

Project STAR

Within such general-population programmes, components can also be designed for the target group – in the case of drugs, children in their pre-teen years. The most successful of these programmes was designed by Mary Ann Pentz and her colleagues and is known as the Midwestern Prevention Program (MPP) or Project STAR – 'Students Taught Awareness and Resistance'. This project tests five interventions under controlled experimental conditions in Kansas City and Indianapolis. The core is the STAR school-based peer-resistance programme. This focuses on the psychosocial consequences of drug abuse. It corrects misinformation; provides training in social resistance skills to offset the pressure to use drugs; gives lessons in assertiveness and problem-solving; and makes a public commitment to avoid using drugs. The rest of the programme is built around this core, including education to encourage better communication between parents and their children, establishing community task groups to promote anti-drug activities, and implementing health policies aimed at eliminating drug use both in schools and in the wider community (for example, creating drug-free zones and no-smoking areas). A mass-media campaign supports all these components.

Research has demonstrated positive long-term effects. Students who began the programme in junior high school, and whose results were measured in their senior high school year, showed significantly less use of cannabis (30% less), cigarettes (25% less) and alcohol (20% less) than children in schools that did not receive the programme (Pentz et al., 1989).

Further analyses of these data by MacKinnon and his colleagues (1991) show that the programme reinforced children's perceptions of the negative effects of drugs. Their friends were more intolerant of drug use, while they were better able to communicate about drugs as well as other problems. The most powerful mediator found to reduce drug use was the increased perception that friends were intolerant of drugs.

Populations at risk

As well as focusing on risk factors and behaviours, many prevention researchers have developed programmes specifically for groups most at risk, such as children of substance abusers or children with behavioural problems. Such interventions are much more direct than those described above.

One example of this type of intervention is the Strengthening Families programme, designed by Karol Kumpfer. This is a multi-component, family-focused programme aimed at six-to-ten-year-old children of substance abusers. There are three elements to the programme:

* parent training (which aims to improve parenting skills and reduce parental substance use);
* children's skills-training (which aims to decrease negative behaviours and increase socially acceptable ones); and
* family skills-training (which allows parents and children to learn and practice their new behaviours and skills).

The programme comprises 14 two-hour weekly sessions. The parents and children are trained separately in the first hour, coming together in the second hour for family training. After multiple assessments, this programme has been found to reduce family conflict, improve family communication and organisation, and reduce youth conduct disorders, aggressiveness and substance abuse (Kumpfer et al., 1996).

A similar programme is the Reconnecting Youth Program, designed by Leona Eggert. Under this scheme, young people in ninth to twelfth grade who have been identified as being 'at risk' are taught skills to increase their resilience to their specific risk factors (whether substance abuse or suicidal tendencies). The programme has been shown to improve school performance, reduce drug involvement, decrease deviant peer bonding, increase self-esteem and social support, and reduce aggression, stress and depression (Eggert *et al.*, 1994).

Overall effectiveness of prevention programmes

Recognising the complexity of the paths that lead towards drug use and abuse has resulted in the development of several broad prevention strategies. Nancy Tobler of the State University of New York has carried out a meta-analysis of 143 evaluated prevention interventions (Tobler, 1992). As a result, she identified five prevention modalities:

* knowledge only;
* affective only;
* peer programmes;
* knowledge plus affective; and
* alternatives.

She then compared the performance of each intervention according to the following desirable outcomes:

* increased knowledge about drugs and their effects;
* changes in attitudes towards drugs and other deviant behaviours;
* decreased or non-use of drugs;
* enhanced refusal, social and life skills; and
* decreased negative behaviours.

Peer programmes had the greatest effect on several outcomes. The enhancement of social skills and assertiveness caused by these programmes was generally found to reduce (or prevent initiation into) drug use. Programmes that offer alternatives to drug use – providing opportunities for recognition and personal achievement through involvement in community or 'self-help' activities – were found to be most effective for those most vulnerable to drug abuse.

In a further analysis, Tobler explored predictors of success in the most effective programmes. Two important factors were found in all of them. First, the nature and content of the programme focused on group interaction; and, second, the programme was conducted by trained mental-health professionals and counsellors.

In addition, age-related strategies appeared to be important. Most effective for children aged 12–14 were strategies that stressed learning interpersonal and refusal skills. These programmes provide information about the social pressures to use drugs and allow the necessary time to practise using these skills. For older children, successful programmes were found to include more structured, drug-focused sessions.

From the above extensive and comprehensive research base, principles or laws for preventing drug abuse can begin to be elucidated. The following preliminary principles address the content, structure and delivery of prevention services.

Prevention principles for children and adolescents

Prevention programmes should:

* be designed to enhance protective factors and attempt to reverse or reduce known risk factors;
* target all forms of drug abuse, including tobacco, alcohol, cannabis and solvents;
* include skills to resist drugs when offered, strengthen personal commitments not to use drugs, and increase social competency (for example, in communication, peer relationships, self-efficacy and assertiveness);
* when targeted at adolescents, include interactive methods, such as peer discussion groups, rather than didactic teaching techniques alone;
* include a component for parents or care-givers that reinforces what the children are learning and that provides opportunities for family discussion since family-focused prevention has a greater impact than strategies that focus solely on parents or children;
* be long term, taking place throughout the school career with repeat interventions to reinforce the original prevention goals – schools offer opportunities to reach all populations and are also important settings for specific 'at-risk' groups;
* strengthen norms against drug use in all drug-abuse prevention settings, including the family, school and the community – as with family interventions, community programmes are more effective when accompanied by school and family components;
* be adapted to address the specific nature of the drug-abuse problem in the local community;
* be more intensive and begin earlier the higher the level of risk experienced by the target population; and
* be age-specific, developmentally appropriate and culturally sensitive.

Future directions

Despite the tremendous achievements of drug-prevention, there remain significant gaps in knowledge. For instance, although much attention has been paid to the efficacy of education, information and other interventions for school-age children, there is still much to be learnt about the influence of the school environment on prevention outcomes. Even today, little is known about how the classroom and school composition influence the effectiveness of interventions. Likewise, very little is known about school policies on drug use, how they vary and how they are implemented. For example, in some schools, children found to be involved with drugs may be expelled, while in others such children may be referred for counselling. What impact such decisions have on school-based drug education remains to be seen. There is also a general belief that drug prevention must begin early in the school career, but there is a dearth of research findings about the effectiveness of earlier exposure to prevention efforts.

Another critical area that requires more work is that of using early 'markers' for later problems. Research suggests that initial indicators of later problem behaviour can be identified as early as elementary school. These markers can include inconsistent and inadequate parenting practices, physical and/or sexual abuse, a low degree of social bonding to family and school, and high levels of sensation seeking. But much more work is needed to understand the relationship between these markers and whether they have any biogenetic base. Special attention should therefore be paid to children of alcoholics and substance abusers. This is one area in which epidemiologists can work more closely with the prevention-intervention researchers to develop reliable risk profiles and protective-factor configurations that predict drug use.

The final gaps to be filled relate to the use of persuasive communication techniques for prevention interventions and the diffusion of this cumulative knowledge to practitioners.

As communications research has become more sophisticated, it has become equally important for prevention practitioners to tailor their message to their specific audience through appropriate channels of communication. But not enough research has been conducted to determine the efficiency and effectiveness of these channels. Also, while the emerging information highway challenges prevention professionals to recognise the advantages of new, multiple ways of reaching audiences, it must also be recognised that competitive, negative uses of those same channels can undermine preventive efforts.

Finally, while prevention research has made much progress in developing and testing new models for family-, school- and community-based programmes, few replication studies validate these programmes, and even fewer test ways of putting them into practice. This is a serious gap and one that prevention researchers are currently trying to address in the United States. The greatest challenge today is to establish the link between research and the community.

References

Altman, J. (1996) 'A biological view of drug abuse', *Molecular Medicine Today*, 2(6), 237–241.

Bachman, J. G., *et al.* (1988) 'Explaining recent decline in marijuana use. Differentiating the effects of perceived risks, disapproval, and general lifestyle factors', *Journal of Health and Social Behavior*, 29(1), 92–112.

Bachman, J. G., *et al.* (1990) 'Explaining the recent decline in cocaine use among young adults. Further evidence that perceived risks and disapproval lead to reduced drug use', *Journal of Health and Social Behavior*, 31(2),173–184.

Bandura, A. (1977) *Social Learning Theory*, Englewood Cliffs, NJ: Prentice Hall.

Botvin, G. (forthcoming) 'Preventing drug abuse through schools: intervention programs that work', in *Proceedings of the National Conference on Drug Abuse Prevention Research Putting Research to Work for the Community.*

Botvin, G., *et al.* (1995) 'Long-term follow-up results of a randomized drug abuse prevention trial in a white middle-class population', *Journal of the American Medical Association*, 273(14), 1106–1112.

Brook, J., *et al.* (1990) 'The psychological etiology of adolescent drug use: A family interactional approach', *Genetic, Social and General Psychology Monographs*, 116(2), 111–267.

Bry, B., and Canby, C. (1986) 'Decreasing adolescent drug use and school failure: long-term effects of targeted family problem-solving training', *Child and Family Behavior Therapy*, 8(1), 43–59.

Cadoret, R., *et al.* (1986) 'An adoption study of genetic and environmental factors in drug abuse', *Archives of General Psychiatry*, 43(12), 1131–1136.

Cassel, J. (1976) 'The contribution of the social environment to host resistance', *American Journal of Epidemiology*, 104(2), 107–123.

Childress, A., *et al.* (1995) 'Limbic activation during cue-induced cocaine craving', *Society for Neuroscience Abstracts*, 21(3), 1956.

Cohen, P., *et al.* (1990) 'Common and uncommon pathways to adolescent psychopathology and problem behaviour', in Robins, L., and Rutter, M. (Eds) *Straight and Devious Pathways from Childhood to Adulthood*, Cambridge: Cambridge University Press.

Demarsh, J., and Kumpfer, K. (1986) 'Family oriented interventions for the prevention of chemical dependency in children and adolescents', in Griswold, S., *et al.* (Eds) *Childhood and Chemical Abuse: Prevention and Intervention*, New York: Haworth.

Dishion, T., and Andrews, D. (1995) 'Preventing escalation in problem behaviors with high-risk young adolescents: immediate and one-year outcomes', *Journal of Consulting and Clinical Psychology*, 63(4), 538–548.

Dishion, T., *et al.* (1996) 'Preventive interventions for high-risk youth: the Adolescent Transitions Program', in Peters, R., and McMahon, R. (Eds) *Preventing Childhood Disorders, Substance Abuse and Delinquency*, Thousand Oaks, CA: Sage.

Dorn, N., and Thompson, A. (1976) 'Evaluation of drug education in the longer term is not an optional extra', *Community Health*, 7(3), 154–161.

Eggert, L., *et al.* (1994) 'Preventing adolescent drug abuse and high school dropout through an intensive school-based social network development program', *American Journal of Health Promotion*, 8(3), 202–215.

Evans, R. (1976) 'Smoking in children: developing a social psychological strategy of deterrence', *Preventive Medicine*, 5(1), 122–127.

Evans, R., *et al.* (1978) 'Deterring the onset of smoking in children: knowledge of immediate physiological effects and coping with peer pressure, media pressure, and parent modeling', *Journal of Applied Social Psychology*, 8(2), 126–135.

Farquhar, J., *et al.* (1990) 'Effects of community-wide education on cardiovascular disease risk factors: the Stanford Five-City Project', *Journal of the American Medical Association*, 264(13), 359–365.

Friedman, A. (1989) 'Family therapy versus parent groups: effects on adolescent drug abusers', *American Journal of Family Therapy*, 17(4), 335–347.

Hansen, W., and Graham, J. (1991) 'Preventing alcohol, marijuana, and cigarette use among adolescents: peer-pressure resistance training versus establishing conservative norms', *Preventive Medicine*, 20(3), 414–430.

Hawkins, J., *et al.* (1992) 'Risk and protective factors for alcohol and other drug problems in adolescence and early adulthood: implications for substance abuse prevention', *Psychological Bulletin*, 112(1), 64–105.

Hirschi, T. (1969) *Causes of Delinquency*, Berkeley, CA: University of California Press.

Jessor, R., and Jessor, S. (1977) *Problem Behavior and Psychosocial Development: A Longitudinal Study of Youth*, New York: Academic Press.

Johnston, L., *et al.* (1996) *National Survey Results on Drug Use from the 'Monitoring the Future' Study, 1975–1995*, Rockville, MD: National Institute on Drug Abuse (NIDA).

Kandel, D., *et al.* (1978) 'Antecedents of adolescent initiation into stages of drug use: a developmental analysis', *Journal of Youth and Adolescence,* 7(1), 13–40.

Kandel, D., *et al.* (1992) 'Stages of progression in drug involvement from adolescence to adulthood: further evidence for the gateway theory', *Journal of Studies on Alcohol*, 53(5), 447–457.

Kaplan, H. (1985) 'Testing a general theory of drug abuse and other deviant adaptations', *Journal of Drug Issues*, 15(4), 477–492.

Kearney, A., and Hines, M. (1980) 'Evaluation of the effectiveness of a drug prevention education program', *Journal of Drug Education*, 10(2), 127–134.

Kim, S. (1988) 'A short- and long-term evaluation of Here's Looking at You. II', *Journal of Drug Education*, 18(3), 235–242.

Kumpfer, K., *et al.* (1996) 'The Strengthening Families Program for the prevention of delinquency and drug use', in Peters, R., and McMahon, R. (Eds) *Preventing Childhood Disorders, Substance Abuse and Delinquency*, Thousand Oaks, CA: Sage.

Lewis, R., *et al.* (1990) 'Family-based interventions for helping drug-using adolescents', *Journal of Adolescent Research*, 5, 82–95.

MacKinnon, D., *et al.* (1991) 'How school-based drug education works: one year effects of the Midwestern Prevention Project', *Health Psychology*, 10(3), 164–172.

McCord, W., and McCord, J. (1959) *Origins of Crime: a New Evaluation of the Cambridge–Somerville Study*, New York: Columbia University Press.

National Institute on Drug Abuse (1996) *Calculations Derived from the 1994 National Household Survey on Drug Abuse by Staff of the Division of Epidemiology and Prevention Research*, Rockville, MD: NIDA.

Newcomb, M., and Bentler, P. (1986) 'Frequency and sequence of drug use: a longitudinal study from early adolescence to young adulthood,' *Journal of Drug Education*, 16(2), 101–120.

O'Donnell, J., *et al.* (1995) 'Preventing school failure, drug use, and delinquency among low-income children: long-term intervention in elementary schools', *American Journal of Orthopsychiatry*, 65(1), 87–100.

Pandina, R. (forthcoming) 'Risk and protective factors in adolescent drug use: putting them to work for prevention', in *Proceedings of the National Conference on Drug Abuse Prevention Research: Putting Research to Work for the Community.*

Pandina, R., and Johnson, V. (1989) 'Familial history as a predictor of alcohol and drug consumption among adolescent children', *Journal of Studies on Alcohol*, 50(3), 245–253.

Patterson, G., *et al.* (1992) *Antisocial Boys*, Eugene, OR: Castalia.

Pentz, M., *et al.* (1989) 'A multi-community trial for primary prevention of adolescent drug abuse: Effects of drug use prevalence', *Journal of the American Medical Association*, 261(22), 3259–3266.

Schaps, E., *et al.* (1981) 'A review of 127 drug abuse prevention program evaluations', *Journal of Drug Issues*, 11(1), 17–43.

Schmidt, S., *et al.* (1996) 'Changes in parenting practices and adolescent drug abuse during multidimensional family therapy', *Journal of Family Psychology*, 10(1), 12–27.

Sechrest, L. (1985) 'Experiments and demonstrations in health services research', *Medical Care*, 23(5), 677–695.

Shedler, J., and Block, J. (1990) 'Adolescent drug use and psychological health: a longitudinal study', *American Psychologist*, 45(5), 612–630.

Swisher, J., and Hoffman, A. (1975) 'Information: the irrelevant variable in drug education', in Corder, B., *et al.* (Eds) *Drug Abuse Prevention: Perspectives and Approaches for Educators*, Dubuque, IA: William C. Brown.

Szapocznik, J., and Kurtines, W. (1989) *Breakthroughs in Family Therapy with Drug-abusing and Problem Youth*, New York: Springer.

Tobler, N. (1992) 'Drug prevention programs can work: research findings', *Journal of Addictive Diseases*, 11(3), 1–28.

Volkow, N., *et al.* (1991) 'Changes in brain glucose metabolism in cocaine dependence and withdrawal', *American Journal of Psychology*, 148(5), 621–626.

Webster-Stratton, C. (1984) 'Randomized trial of two-parent training programs for families with conduct disordered children', *Journal of Consulting and Clinical Psychology*, 52(4), 666–678.

Webster-Stratton, C. (1990) 'Enhancing the effectiveness of self-administered videotape parent training for families with conduct problem children', *Journal of Abnormal Child Psychology*, 18(5), 479–492.

Winkleby, M., *et al.* (1994) 'A community-based heart disease intervention: predictors of change', *American Journal of Public Health*, 84(5), 767–772.

CHAPTER 3

BARRIERS AND CHALLENGES TO EVALUATION

Teresa Salvador-Llivina

The purpose of this chapter is not to review why the drug-prevention field should adopt the practice of evaluation. However, the benefits that sound evaluation can bring to the field must be borne in mind. Despite current efforts, prevention intervention is still a relatively new discipline, and only a few proven interventions and a limited knowledge base exist. In this context, the grounds for conducting evaluations become both more urgent and more attractive. The following arguments for evaluation have been advanced by a number of authors (Hawkins and Nederhood, 1987; Klitzner and Stewart, 1990; Green and Kreuter, 1991; Kumpfer *et al.*, 1993; Muraskin, 1993):

* To determine whether an intervention effectively addresses its stated objectives.
* To verify, document and quantify activities and their effects.
* To allow the intervention's efficacy and efficiency to be improved.
* To provide a rational basis for decision-making.
* To facilitate informed choices between the different approaches available.
* To provide feedback and systematic assessment to staff about their job performance.
* To provide a positive forum in which to discuss operational issues that might otherwise remain hidden and lead to staff burn-out.
* To act as positive reinforcement for those involved in programme-planning and implementation.
* To increase public awareness.
* To add credibility to or legitimise programmes, both technically and politically.

Many other benefits of evaluation could be added to this list, but this chapter deals instead with exactly the opposite – the problems that must be faced and addressed in order to root evaluation firmly within the prevention field.

The first problem in discussing evaluation is one of the general themes of this monograph – the diversity of meanings. The very word 'evaluation' means different things to different people. For politicians, the main purpose of evaluation might be to increase social well-being, control budgets and raise their own electoral popularity. For programme staff, however, evaluation might represent an ethical responsibility to ensure that their approach is 'sound', while success, of course, grants them professional recognition and promotes their prospects. Evaluators and researchers, on the other hand, may simply see evaluation in terms of promoting 'good practice' and doing their job well.

All these can be the right reasons if, at the same time, evaluation ultimately leads to improvements in current interventions and serves as a useful tool with which to plan future interventions.

The following sections analyse in greater detail some of the main non-methodological factors that can interfere in, or create difficulties for, any evaluation process.

Down to earth: the context of evaluation

Some determining factors need to be considered before the main obstacles to planning and implementing an evaluation can be described.

Decision-making and allocating resources

For nearly two decades, it has been recognised in Europe that the effectiveness of prevention interventions should be monitored. Yet implementing evaluation fully remains a complex task. The literature shows that evaluating outcomes in general, and medium- and long-term follow-ups in particular, is given a low priority in planning and funding an intervention.

The theoretical recognition of the need for evaluation is counterbalanced by a practical lack of European interventions that have been evaluated (see, for example, European Prevention Assessment System, 1994; Hanewinkel, 1994; European Commission, 1994; Künzel-Böhmer et al., 1994; Salvador-Llivina and Ware, 1995). One study that compared national policies in the European Union found that research into the efficacy of prevention interventions is not defined as a priority in any Member State (Centro de Estudios sobre la Promoción de la Salud, 1995). With such a lack of political support, it is extremely difficult to 'normalise' evaluation as an essential part of prevention.

Countries should, therefore, urgently consider including evaluation as a condition sine qua non for implementing prevention interventions, and a percentage of the drug budget should be set aside for systematic evaluations. Without such a commitment, any progress relies on the voluntary efforts of prevention professionals, and will, therefore, often suffer from instability and burn-out.

Internal versus external evaluation

In principle, the choice of internal or external evaluation should depend on the questions the evaluation seeks to answer. It must be remembered that evaluation is a specialised task requiring highly developed skills, such as experience of experimental designs, statistics, psychometry and data processing. Ideally, the evaluator will also have a comprehensive knowledge of drug prevention, its methodology and practice. External evaluators who meet these criteria, and who are properly integrated with the implementation team, can help to ensure objective and high-quality evaluations and outcomes.

In practice, the choice of internal or external evaluation normally depends on the level of financial support available. Expertise is expensive and most current interventions cannot afford it. Recognising the scarcity of resources devoted to evaluation, it may be more realistic to ask 'who could?' rather than 'who should?' undertake the evaluation. This, then, raises the question: how can good evaluation be facilitated by evaluators who are not experts?

Taking these constraints into account, providing implementation teams with easy-to-use methods and protocols that enable them to monitor, at least to a certain extent, their own activities must be considered. This raises new issues, such as the allocation of resources to training budgets and the distinction between being evaluated and conducting an evaluation. Only when these are answered by the field as a whole can a viable model be drawn up to normalise evaluation within the prevention sector.

The basic distinction between evaluation and research

The 'technology-transfer' approach sees evaluation as an essential element of the scientific process. From this perspective, prevention methodologies and interventions grow from research into application, and evaluation is based on controlled trials that allow the programme to be further tested and, hopefully, lead to the eventual widespread adoption of the intervention in non-research settings (Schinke and Orlandi, 1991).

Table 1

Technology-transfer stages	Drug-abuse prevention stages
1. Basic research	Theory development; data synthesis
2. Applied research	Case study; clinical work; exploratory studies
3. Technology development	Construction of intervention curricula
4. Evaluation	Clinical trials; analogue and outcome
5. Demonstration	Field studies with evaluation; focus on population
6. Adoption	Use in non-research settings
7. Application in practice	Widespread acceptance and use of intervention among line practitioners
8. Obsolescence	Disuse of old intervention technology; evolution to a new technology

Source: Schinke and Orlandi, 1991

However, reality is more complex than the neat technology-transfer approach suggests. In practice, the rationale for a prevention intervention comes not just from empirically based data, but also from social perceptions and public demands. Thus, it is also necessary to make a basic distinction between research and evaluation.

The nature of descriptive and explanatory research

Research is the only tool that can definitively establish causal relations and identify outcomes. It does so by maintaining controlled conditions. However, research usually only adds to knowledge over a long period of time. There are broadly two types of research.

Descriptive research is essentially practice-based, relying on observation, allowing for population-based trends, and estimating national, regional and local prevalence and incidence of drug use. It also helps to define the characteristics of those who use drugs, and identifies risk factors and other conditions associated with drug misuse. This assists in developing causal hypotheses as well as identifying consequences.

Explanatory research, on the other hand, is based on causal rationales and calls for explanations – hypotheses, tests, methodology and controlled trials (Howard, 1990). The ultimate purpose of such research is to define the components of effective interventions – by measuring intermediate and ultimate outcomes – as well as to validate any causal relationships. Furthermore, explanatory research is above all theory-based, allowing generalisations to be made from one intervention to another, even though their setting may vary. This incrementally builds up the knowledge base.

Formative and summative evaluation

Evaluation is a very particular form of research that is intended to assess the results of a non-experimental intervention. As such, and unlike laboratory research, evaluations must cope with the uncertainty of real life (Rossi and Freeman, 1989). As a recent report stresses (Centre for Substance Abuse Prevention, 1993), evaluations can therefore suffer from many uncontrollable conditions:

* mid-stream changes in the intervention, leading to new measures of process and outcome and, usually, a revised evaluation design;
* changes in 'site' participation (entire schools dropping out, for instance), distorting the initial research design;
* poor retention and high attrition rates at the individual level, that may jeopardise statistical analysis and the evaluation results in general; and
* strained relationships between the evaluation and implementation teams, frequently reflecting different professional incentives, systems and goals.

Despite these challenges, evaluation as a tool for developing knowledge makes two major contributions. First, its findings can be used directly by the implementation team to help them improve their interventions (the by-now familiar concept of 'formative evaluation' – Scriven, 1967). Second, 'summative evaluation' allows policy-makers to make wide-ranging and long-term assessments of interventions in general.

In this context, then, evaluation's primary goal is to further knowledge and increase feedback about the implementation process. Unlike research, it can also pilot new ideas in the field. This distinction between research and evaluation is vital. If evaluation is to be normalised, it must be flexible – practitioners, teachers, parents and youth workers everywhere will simply not (and quite rightly) conduct a controlled trial every time they want to prevent drug misuse. The fear that research strikes into people sometimes means that nothing is done. Research can also scare people into believing that evaluation is an impossible task. The challenge is to promote evaluation as necessary and ultimately useful.

Common problems in evaluating prevention

It is difficult to discuss in the abstract the problems faced during an evaluation. The evaluation process will encounter different obstacles depending on its origin – whether it emerged from within the programme, or was foisted on it from outside. The process may also vary depending on who conducts the evaluation. Without attempting a comprehensive analysis of all potential situations, this section outlines some of the most frequent problems faced during evaluations.

Prior problems

Despite its value, evaluation is not always welcomed. Often, a planned evaluation must overcome several barriers before it becomes part of a programme. Many obstacles arise simply out of fear, the most common being that the data provided by the evaluation will reveal a fatal flaw in the programme. This derives from a basic misunderstanding of the potential of evaluation to guide programme activities and goals. Klitzner and Stewart (1990) suggest that the most common fears are:

* that evaluation poses a threat to those with an investment in the intervention's success;
* that an evaluation may interfere in other activities; and
* that resources otherwise allocated to programme activities will be diverted.

A further fear is that the evaluation outcomes will be manipulated by parties who wish the intervention to fail and will be used to justify long-standing decisions, such as budget cuts, sackings or postponing certain projects.

Process problems

Once the above obstacles are overcome, the actual implementation of the evaluation itself frequently creates further problems that need to be anticipated and tackled appropriately.

Many of these problems are methodological (for example, the difficulties encountered when seeking a valid sample or ensuring that intermediate variables are monitored). These aspects have already been discussed in previous chapters. Other problems with implications for the success or failure of an evaluation go beyond methodological issues and relate to the practical aspects of implementation.

Institutional problems

This refers to difficulties raised within the organisation that is implementing the evaluation. The most likely institutional problem is that the evaluation will create an understandable resistance to change. Classic institutional inertia could halt a need for change because implementing the new practices requires investment (in time, resources or manpower) which is not possible at the time. Furthermore, the required changes could be seen as unacceptable because they conflict with current institutional expectations or with institutional values, and the potential changes could ultimately be incompatible with the institution's ideology, thus threatening its very *raison d'être*.

Interpersonal problems

Another group of problems can derive from interpersonal conflicts. Evaluators may be greeted with a certain degree of distrust or non-cooperation, especially when the evaluation is external. While the project-implementers are likely to be concerned with clients and the 'here and now', professional evaluators can have a 'colder' approach to the situation, one that may not endear them to the project workers. Another philosophical point of departure is that practitioners often have a messianic belief in what they are doing, while evaluators systematically question every aspect of their work. The roots of this may, on the one hand, be the practitioner's fear of the evaluator, and, on the other, arrogance on the part of the evaluator.

Technical problems

Many technical difficulties can interfere with the implementation of an evaluation. The most frequent ones are:

* *Inadequacies in the terms of reference.* Before implementing an evaluation plan, terms of reference should be drawn up so that all involved know exactly what is to be achieved and how success is to be measured. These terms of reference should be clearly defined during the planning phase, as any weakness can lead to serious shortcomings in the quality of the whole process. Should the method- ology be inappropriate, the assessment will be based on false assumptions and the conclusions will be unsatisfactory.

   The most serious mistakes tend to be made when goals are being defined. The objectives of any evaluation are the key to how successful the process will be. All too frequently, however, the aims are unclear or open to different interpretations. Without well-defined objectives, any measurement will be very difficult. If an objective cannot be measured, evaluation is impossible.

* *Incompatible evaluative needs and models.* A poor choice of evaluative model can cause serious problems for the procedure. It is all too easy to fall into the trap of using over-sophisticated tools when simpler ones would suffice, and vice versa. Similarly, if an evaluator is collecting information using inaccurate instruments and the wrong methodology, the results will be founded on misleading information and therefore lead to the wrong conclusions.

* *Lack of technical expertise in the evaluation team.* It is vital that the evaluation team use a statistical consultant to review the model and plans, thus ensuring that they are appropriately matched. Without such consultation, the analysis may, once again, reach unsustainable conclusions.

Operational problems

The practical implementation of the evaluation can also create conflict and difficulty. The most common problems are:

* *Inappropriate dissemination of evaluation results.* Using any unofficial channel to distribute initial evaluation results (leaking results to people who had no responsibility for the intervention) should be avoided as it creates irregular and often unmanageable situations.
* *Inappropriate timing in reporting the results.* An evaluation's results are often communicated to funders and executive bodies after decisions have been made about the intervention's future. There may be many valid excuses for such a lack of co-ordination, but results clearly cannot be used if they have been presented late.

Problems can also arise when only one aspect is emphasised in the initial release of the evaluation results. This will negatively affect, and certainly bias, any further decision-making processes.

Challenges for the future

All the difficulties discussed above, although daunting, are not insurmountable. Obstacles can instead be turned into challenges and barriers into opportunities.

Overcoming fear

Some of the fears discussed above relate to negative results and having no control over their use. Evaluators must be aware of these fears, and accordingly ensure that their evaluation reports become useful management tools (Springer, 1990). In other words, evaluators are responsible for finding ways to make evaluation serve interventions and not jeopardise them. Evaluation has to become a constructive management tool, if not a trusted companion for interventions (Centre for Substance Abuse Prevention, 1993).

Experience suggests that the fear of evaluation can be reduced by including project managers and staff in the planning process. Their contributions should be sought from the beginning, and they should be given an active role in interpreting the results.

Facing institutional barriers

Before evaluation planning begins – that is, before engaging in a process that might suggest changes to the programme itself – the project's capacity to implement structural or functional alterations should be analysed. This analysis should consider other 'shaping' factors, such as political aspects, the financial situation and even group psychology. By undertaking this simple analysis of what is possible, an organisation can be spared engaging in a costly process which might lead to inapplicable results.

By simply talking to programme-managers, evaluators can also discover a great deal about the characteristics of a particular institutional environment, as well as the institution's ability to absorb change.

In the final analysis, evaluators should be realistic, keeping proposals for change within the realms of the possible. If there is any doubt about the capacity for institutional change, the evaluators should suggest several alternative measures to deal with the problem. In this way, decision-makers will be able to opt for the most suitable measures.

Dealing with interpersonal misunderstanding

Given the characteristics of the relationship between evaluator and evaluated, it is very difficult to eliminate totally all sources of conflict. However, some measures can help to reduce these conflicts as much as possible (Espinoza Vergara, 1986). For example, evaluators can share and clarify the evaluation's objectives with the participants. Such pooling of ideas can enrich the final evaluation. Furthermore, co-operation between practitioners and evaluators can be enhanced by involving all parties in discussions about the evaluation's objectives. Finally, evaluators should avoid overloading participants with too many commitments. Programme-managers and staff are weighed down with work at the best of times, and evaluation should not add to their burden.

Dealing with unexpected results

High-quality outcome evaluations should be designed to verify, document and quantify programme activities and their effects. This information can both determine any unintended effects (whether negative or positive) and identify factors separate from the intervention that could have affected the outcomes. This is why programme teams should learn not to fear unexpected results – they can be beneficial and can even provide alternative explanations for an apparently failing intervention.

Gottfredson *et al.* (1990), for instance, reported that a group-counselling intervention was actually found to increase rather than decrease involvement with drugs. Fortunately, however, the authors had collected additional information that demonstrated that the unintended outcome was in fact due to an increase in negative peer pressure within the group because only 'at-risk' young people were included in the intervention (Kumpfer *et al.*, 1993). This clearly illustrates the relevance of differentiating 'results' from evaluation 'findings'. In other words, identifying negative results and their causes is crucial if practitioners and evaluators are to learn about unforeseen influences and be able to suggest changes that will improve the programme's effectiveness.

Identifying a programme's weaknesses is just as important as identifying its strengths. If impacts are not measured in a valid manner, or are hidden because negative consequences are too unpalatable, then evaluation results will not help improve a programme – which should, after all, be the ultimate purpose of any evaluation.

Improving reporting procedures

The presentation of the evaluation results and the link between their availability and future decision-making processes are the final keys to an evaluation's success.

The assessment report should be given to all those who request it, and – as discussed above – the evaluators should also avoid presenting partial material that could be misunderstood. The completed report must be available in good time so that informed decisions can be made. This means that the evaluation must finish on schedule. In the real world, of course, delays do happen, but when they do, decision-makers should be informed and any major decisions postponed until accurate evaluation information is available.

The other crucial issue that the final report raises is 'where do we go from here?' Too often, evaluative reports end up on an office shelf. Clearly, the recommendations must be acted upon immediately (although this does not mean that they have to be *implemented* immediately). Speed is of the essence, and although decision-making processes are generally slow, it must be impressed upon all involved that social processes – such as the pressure to take drugs – move quickly.

European co-operation to facilitate evaluation

There are no magic solutions to the complex problems of prevention evaluation. The challenge today is to convince politicians of the need for evaluation. Prevention evaluation is unlikely to be greatly advanced without the systematic allocation of resources.

The recession of the early 1990s has meant that social services in many European countries have experienced dramatic cutbacks. More than ever, this calls for evaluation to eliminate naïve and ineffective activities. At the same time, the real costs of evaluation need to be lowered.

The European Union can play a key role in normalising evaluation. European institutions can act as a forum for agreeing a set of evaluation standards that can save time and money – and lives. One of the goals of the Union's five-year Programme of Community Action on the Prevention of Drug Dependence is the development of 'a strategy for research on the use of appropriate techniques for preventive purposes'. This present monograph, and the accompanying *Guidelines for the Evaluation of Drug Prevention*, are successful examples of the European effort to promote this strategy.

On the other hand, the Member States are not starting from scratch. Most European countries already have isolated but effective experiences of evaluation, and well-trained professionals can help to create national policies on evaluation.

Finally, new and imaginative strategies must be explored and tested so that existing evaluative resources can be used efficiently. Co-operation with research institutes and universities could provide the key to cheaper evaluation (Ferrer-Pérez, 1985), while co-ordinating disparate programmes can help to reduce investment in manpower, materials, dissemination of good practice and the development of measurement instruments.

References

Center for Substance Abuse Prevention (CSAP) (1993) *Progress Report. Learning About the Effects of Alcohol and Other Drug Abuse Prevention*, Rockville, MD: CSAP.

Centro de Estudios sobre la Promoción de la Salud (CEPS) (1995), 'Comparative study on drug abuse prevention policies of the Member States of the European Union. Background information', in *Conference on Drugs Policy in Europe*, Brussels: European Commission.

Espinoza Vergara, M. (1986) *Evaluación de Proyectos Sociales*, Buenos Aires: Humanitas.

European Commission (1994) 'Integrated approach and general directions of the European Union's action to combat drugs (1995–1999)', unpublished report.

European Prevention Assessment System (EPAS) (1994) *COPE*, Madrid: EPAS.

Ferrer-Pérez, X. (1985) 'La evaluación de là prevención del abuso de drogas', Paper presented at the 'XII Jornadas Nacionales de Socidrogalcohol', Palma de Mallorca.

Gottfredson, D., *et al.* (1990) *Compendium of Instruments to Measure Drug Use and Risk Factors for Drug Use,* Baltimore, MD: Johns Hopkins University Press.

Green, L., and Kreuter, M. (1991) *Health Promotion Planning. An Educational and Environmental Approach*, Mountain View, CA: Mayfield Publishing.

Hanewinkel, R. (1994) 'Methods of evaluating primary prevention measures', Paper presented at the Seminar 'Evaluation of Primary Prevention', International Congress on the Occasion of European Prevention Week, Aachen.

Hawkins, D., and Nederhood, B. (1987) *Handbook for Evaluating Drug and Alcohol Prevention Programs*, Rockville, MD: CSAP.

Howard, J. (1990) 'Prevention research at NIAAA: confronting the challenge of uncertainty', in Rey, K., *et al.* (Eds) *Prevention Research Findings*, Rockville, MD: CSAP.

Klitzner, M., and Stewart, K. (1990) *Evaluating Faculty Development and Clinical Training Programs in Substance Abuse: A Guide Book*, Bethesda, MD: Pacific Institute for Research and Evaluation.

Kumpfer, K., *et al.* (1993) *Measurements in Prevention. A Manual on Selecting and Using Instruments to Evaluate Prevention Programs*, Rockville, MD: CSAP.

Künzel-Böhmer, J., *et al.* (1994) *Expert Report on Primary Prevention of Substance Abuse*, Munich: Institut für Therapieforschung.

Muraskin, L. (1993) *Understanding Evaluation: The Way to Better Prevention Programs*, Washington DC: Westat, Inc., and US Department of Education.

Rossi, P., and Freeman, H. (1989) *Evaluation: A Systematic Approach*, 4th edition, Newbury Park, CA: Sage.

Salvador-Llivina, T., and Ware, S. (1995) 'Drug abuse prevention policies and research in Europe: notes for a future agenda', *Drugs: Education, Prevention and Policy*, 2(1), 7–15.

Schinke, S., and Orlandi, M. (1991) 'Technology Transfer', in National Institute on Drug Abuse (NIDA) (Ed.) *Drug Abuse Prevention Intervention Research: Methodological Issues*, Rockville, MD: NIDA.

Scriven, M. (1967) 'The methodology of evaluation', in American Educational Research Association (AERA) (Ed.) *Perspectives on Curriculum Evaluation*, Chicago, IL: Rand McNally.

Springer, J. (1990) 'Learning from prevention policy: A management-focused approach', in Rey, K., *et al.* (Eds) *Prevention Research Findings*, Rockville, MD: CSAP.

EVALUATION
IN PRACTICE

Part II examines the issue of evaluation in detail. In Chapter 4, Christoph Kröger presents the conceptual basis of evaluation. He briefly sketches the different types and aspects of evaluation before examining the diversity and complexity of a number of prevention-evaluation models in more detail.

Thomas Jertfelt then tackles the practicalities of evaluation and the very real problems of ensuring that an evaluation report is taken seriously. Any evaluation must be accepted as a tool for future work, and so it is crucial for all the parties involved to reach a common understanding of an evaluation's processes and findings. In other words, the author concludes, effective evaluation requires public relations and communication skills just as much as it requires scientific knowledge.

In Chapter 6, Han Kuipers examines one of evaluation's more complex methodological issues – that of 'mediating variables'. According to the author, these factors, which can influence drug use, are key to the success or failure of a drug-prevention intervention. If a programme targets mediating variables that are causally related to drug use, then that drug-use behaviour can be changed. The difficulty, of course, is to isolate the 'right' mediating variable, and by analysing a number of theoretical models that have been tested in the field, Kuipers gives some examples of how to do so.

Mark Morgan's chapter discusses the development and implementation of evaluation instruments. Many of these are similar to those used in epidemiological research, such as inconsistent application. In many cases, developing evaluation instruments is assumed to be a simple task, an assumption that has led to the use of inappropriate instruments, making comparisons between studies difficult. The author argues that structured questionnaires are among the best ways to measure evaluation outcomes.

In Chapter 8, Christine Godfrey and Steve Parrott examine the issue of cost-effectiveness in drug-prevention programmes. Economic evaluation is a well-established field, and the authors propose adapting existing guidelines for drug prevention. Godfrey and Parrott outline the questions that economic evaluation techniques could address, as well as the different types of economic evaluations and the situations in which they can be applied most appropriately. The authors also compare the different types of cost and benefit that can be used in an economic evaluation of a drug-prevention initiative, and outline the steps necessary to undertake such an evaluation.

Finally, Richard Hartnoll discusses how the science of epidemiology can be of practical value to drug prevention and prevention-evaluation research. Using concrete examples and models, he demonstrates how epidemiological analysis can help in assessing problems and needs related to established and problematic drug use, and in identifying new trends. However, the tools that epidemiology offers have not always been fully exploited in prevention and prevention research, and Hartnoll concludes by proposing closer links between epidemiology and prevention, research and practice.

CHAPTER 4

EVALUATION: DEFINITIONS AND CONCEPTS

Christoph Kröger

It is clear from the literature on prevention that the term 'evaluation' has no single meaning. Indeed, there sometimes appear to be as many definitions and classifications as there are handbooks and evaluators. The phrase 'evaluating prevention interventions' is therefore misleading, as it suggests that there is only one type of evaluation. Yet, over the last few years, many individuals and organisations have been working towards a single concept of 'evaluation'.

In 1993, the European Commission's COST-A6 working group on evaluating prevention held a series of expert meetings and published a Delphi study in an attempt to define primary prevention and its evaluation. The result of all this work has been a comprehensive overview of how to classify prevention evaluation. This classification is, perhaps, the best place to begin (Uhl, 1997a and 1997b).

Evaluating process and outcome

The most commonly accepted definition of 'evaluation' distinguishes between 'process', 'outcome' and 'impact'.

Process evaluation refers to the systematic recording of data during an intervention. It examines all the work carried out by the project staff and the reactions of the target population, asking why and how an intervention achieves its results. It does not, however, evaluate those results.

Outcome evaluation begins where 'process' ends – after an intervention has taken place. It tests whether, and to what extent, the expected results materialised, and attempts to answer the fundamental question of whether the intervention was 'successful'. Outcome evaluation is what most people understand evaluation to be.

Impact evaluation records how the intervention affected people and places beyond the defined targets and target groups. It looks for unexpected effects, the generalisation of effects, and the negative as well as the positive impacts of an intervention.

Generally, little distinction is made between outcome and impact evaluation as both look at the effects of a given intervention. The term 'outcome evaluation' is, therefore, commonly used to describe all the effects of an intervention. However, it is vital to separate process and outcome evaluation, as this creates the framework for many other evaluation terms and definitions.

Other concepts extend the process–outcome model to include creating and planning the intervention.

Formative and summative evaluation

Another frequently used classification distinguishes between 'formative' and 'summative' evaluation (Liedekerken *et al.*, 1990; Uhl, 1997b).

Formative evaluation takes place during the development and piloting of a new intervention. It may give some insights into effectiveness and efficiency, as it follows an intervention from the very beginning to its final implementation.

Summative evaluation begins once the intervention has been developed. It attempts to assess the overall effects of the intervention and asks whether certain effects can actually be achieved. This type of evaluation is often used to decide whether an intervention should be continued or stopped.

Formative and summative evaluation also differ methodologically and epistemologically.

Classification by methodology

Evaluation implies the systematic application of social-science research methods to provide a criterion by which to classify evaluation (Rossi, Freeman and Hofmann, 1988). 'Experimental', 'quasi-experimental' and 'non-experimental' designs can be distinguished.

Experimental designs employ a 'control group' as well as the 'experimental group'. Each condition being examined must use both groups, with the experimental group receiving the intervention, and the control groups either not receiving it, or receiving an irrelevant intervention. All groups are pre-tested and post-tested, and are randomly assigned to the experimental or control condition.

Quasi-experimental designs are identical to 'true' experimental designs except that the groups are not randomly, but deliberately assigned to the different conditions.

Non-experimental designs investigate only one experimental group. Data can be collected either before and after the intervention, or only afterwards.

Data quality

The quality of the data collected is yet another way to categorise evaluation. 'Quantitative' and 'qualitative' studies differ in terms of the instruments used to collect evaluation data.

Qualitative studies rely on interviews and field observation for their data. They deal flexibly with data analysis in order to generate new ideas, hypotheses and theories. These studies present their results descriptively.

Quantitative studies use standardised data-collection instruments that deliver so-called 'hard' (empirically based) data. These studies tend to have experimental designs and apply complex statistical analysis. Experimentally designed quantitative models are used to test hypotheses and verify theories.

Epistemological aims

Deciding which method to choose is closely related to the epistemological aim of a particular evaluation – is it simply to document an intervention, or to broaden the field's knowledge base? Three paradigms of the epistemological approach have been identified (Uhl, 1997a).

Descriptive evaluation deals with monitoring, documenting and summarising an intervention. It does not attempt to discover new phenomena or to formulate new hypotheses.

Exploratory evaluation, on the other hand, attempts to develop new ideas and theories. It does not test hypotheses, and the results are therefore preliminary.

Confirmatory evaluation sets out to test hypotheses, using commonly accepted methods (control-group designs, empirical data analysis, and so on).

Phase models

Many classifications of evaluation focus on the development or genesis of an intervention. The distinction between formative and summative evaluation is the basis for these classifications, two of which are described below.

The Herman model

Herman, Morris and Fitz-Gibbon (1989) distinguish four hypothetical phases in an intervention's life: initiation; planning; implementation; and accountability.

The development of any programme begins with its *initiation*. This stage identifies the goals to be accomplished and the needs to be addressed. Evaluation at this stage helps programme-developers focus their efforts.

In the *planning* phase, controlled piloting and market testing can be undertaken to assess the effectiveness and feasibility either of a new programme or of a pre-existing one.

Implementation describes the execution of the programme. Evaluation during this phase (corresponding to formative evaluation) covers implementation and assesses the operation of the programme. These efforts allow the intervention to be improved.

Finally, *accountability* begins once the programme is established. The main aim is to prove the effectiveness and impact of the intervention, and the evaluation here corresponds to summative evaluation.

The Uhl model

According to Uhl (1997a and 1997b), the process of creating and evaluating a programme can be divided into five stages: basic research; prevention research; programme development; controlled implementation; and final implementation with routine application.

Developing a programme begins with *basic research*. This covers all research areas relevant to the development of any intervention, although it does not cover prevention itself. These basic research areas include addiction research, developmental and social psychology, epidemiology, social marketing and developing assessment tools.

At the *prevention-research* stage, models and theories are developed to describe the initiation, maintenance, reduction and cessation of substance misuse.

The results of both basic and prevention research form the basis for the development and evaluation of a prevention programme.

During *programme development* (corresponding to the formative phase), the intervention is planned and evaluation begins. Ideally, as a first step, preliminary programmes are developed and evaluated in pre-tests and pilot studies, then are modified and finalised into an intervention that is ready to be used in the field without major problems.

After a programme has been finalised, its usefulness is confirmed by *controlled implementation*. At this stage, feasibility and efficiency should systematically be tested under controlled conditions.

The *final implementation and routine application* begin once the effectiveness of the programme has been demonstrated. At this stage, further proof of effectiveness is not central, and it is more important to ensure that the programme is carried out to a high standard. The intervention's implementation is monitored, as are unexpected positive or negative effects and any changes in the situation which may affect implementation.

Implementation-focused models

Many classifications of evaluation are based on the process–outcome model, focusing on implementing a prevention intervention. Two such models are described below.

The Rossi–Freeman model

Rossi and Freeman (Rossi *et al.*, 1979 and 1982) have produced a model based on process–outcome that includes programme planning and differentiates between the evaluations of each phase. They identify four types of evaluation research for: programme planning; monitoring implementation; assessing impact; and measuring efficiency.

The first type of evaluation, *programme-planning* research, is essential for any new intervention or for major modifications in pre-existing ones. It attempts to answer the following questions:

* What is the extent and scale of the problem and who is the target population?
* Has the programme been designed in line with its intended goals, and have the chances of successful implementation been maximised?

Monitoring programme implementation checks whether the actual implementation corresponds to the programme design. The following questions are relevant:

* Is the programme reaching the target group?
* Is the programme providing the intended resources, services and other benefits?

Impact assessment monitors the programme's effectiveness. Questions to ask could be:

* Is the programme achieving its intended results?
* Can these results be explained by any other process unrelated to the programme?

The key concepts of *measuring efficiency* are cost–benefit analysis and cost-effectiveness analysis (see Chapter 8). Relevant questions are:

* What are the costs of delivering the service and the benefits to the programme participants?
* Does the programme make the best use of available resources compared to alternative uses?

A modified model published in 1982 distilled the four phases into three themes: programme concept and design; monitoring and accountability of implementation; and assessment of programme utility.

The Kok model

Kok and Jonkers (1986) stress the importance of the planning stage. Their model contains five steps in both the planning and evaluation phases. They link the relationship between planning and evaluation by using the same keywords for both phases.

The five steps in the planning phase are:

* to identify the specific problem to be tackled;
* to identify the relationship between the problem and the problem behaviour;
* to identify the determinants and causes of the behaviour;
* based on this determinant analysis, to identify an appropriate intervention; and
* to decide how to implement the intervention.

In the evaluation phase, the following five steps can be followed:

* to describe the course of the implementation;
* to describe how the intervention was carried out,
* to describe the effects of the intervention on the determinants of behaviour;
* to describe the effects of the intervention on the behaviour itself; and
* to assess how far the intervention has contributed to solving the problem.

Conclusion

As should by now be apparent, two basic concepts form the core of the scientific evaluation models described: process–outcome evaluation; and formative–summative evaluation. Both concepts differ in the way they look at a programme to be evaluated. The process–outcome model focuses on the process of *implementation*, while the formative–summative model focuses on the process of *creating* and *developing* an intervention.

It should also be clear that the literature describes numerous different models, which rarely employ any common terminology – and when they do, the same terms are often used differently. For example, the term 'outcome evaluation' can be used in a very specific sense (dealing only with the defined objectives and expected results) or in a very broad sense, covering all the outcomes. Likewise, the same process will have a different name in different models such as 'accountability', 'effectiveness' or 'impact' – when in fact all that is different is the researcher's own perspective.

These phantom distinctions are carried through into different kinds of evaluation – quantitative and qualitative approaches, it is argued, exclude each other, while exploratory and confirmatory studies cannot both be carried out. But in reality, as all evaluations share the same goal of extending knowledge about a particular intervention, there are more similarities between them than the different models suggest. The encouraging sign is that, whatever model or terminology an evaluator chooses, there is, overall, an overwhelming consensus on what evaluation is for.

References

Herman, J., Morris, L., and Fitz-Gibbon, C. (1989) *Evaluator's Handbook*, Beverley Hills, CA: Sage.

Kok, G., and Jonkers, R. (1986) 'Gvo en preventie', in *Gvo/aggz Preventie Reader*, Utrecht: Landelijk Centrum Gvo.

Liedekerken, P., *et al.* (1990) *Effectiveness of Health Education*, Utrecht: Dutch Health Education Centre.

Rossi, P., Freeman, H., and Hofmann, G. (1988) *Programm-Evaluation. Einführung in die Methoden angewandter Sozialforschung*, Stuttgart: Enke.

Rossi, P., Freeman, H., and Rosenbaum, S. (1982) *Evaluation. A Systematic Approach*, 2nd edition, Beverley Hills, CA: Sage.

Rossi, P., Freeman, H., and Wright, S. (1979) *Evaluation. A Systematic Approach*, Beverley Hills, CA: Sage.

Uhl, A. (1997a) 'Probleme bei der Evaluation von Präventionsmaßnahmen im Suchtbereich', *Wiener Zeitschrift für Suchtforschung*, 20(34), 93–109.

Uhl, A. (1997b) 'Evaluation of primary prevention in the field of illicit drugs. Definitions – concepts – problems', in Springer, A., and Uhl, A. (Eds) *Evaluation Research in Regard to Primary Prevention of Drug Abuse*, COST A-6, Brussels: Commission of the European Communities.

CHAPTER 5

EVALUATION PLANNING

Thomas Jertfelt

There are two approaches to designing any evaluation: the scientific; and the outcome. The *scientific* approach concerns those parts of the evaluation that deal, for instance, with methods, samples and interpreting statistics. Some of these aspects are described elsewhere in this monograph. This chapter focuses on the *outcome* of an evaluation or, to be more specific, its 'acceptance'. It must, however, be stressed that the scientific standard is the basis for accepting any evaluation. Put more simply, an evaluation succeeds or fails depending on its methodology.

If the evaluation is viewed as a piece of work in its own right and as a springboard to a new understanding of how to improve a particular intervention, and not (as so often) simply as a summary and justification of already-completed work, then it soon becomes clear that an evaluation must be acceptable as a tool for future use. There are many crucial points in the evaluation process, but, ultimately, if the conclusions and recommendations are accepted by the principal actors involved, then the evaluation can play a positive role.

Planning the evaluation is one such crucial point. At this stage – and with the participation of the main actors – the ground is prepared for the evaluation and its conclusions to be ultimately accepted. In other words, the success or otherwise of the evaluation not only depends on its scientific integrity, but also on how it is received. It could, indeed, be said that the evaluation should not be seen simply as a 'narrative', explaining the situation, but as an instrument for developing future prevention activities.

There is nothing worse than an ignored evaluation. Therefore, from the very beginning of the planning process, the evaluation's outcome must be prepared pragmatically to make it acceptable to those who will continue the preventive efforts.

Fundamental planning issues

This section examines, first, the evaluation's more technical aspects and, second, its more process-oriented ones. The two, however, cannot function without each other – some technical elements drive the process-oriented ones.

Each and every evaluation share a number of objectives. These can include:

* outcomes, relating to the initial objectives and the final target group;
* what actually happened;

- why it happened;
- the results of different activities;
- the possible future outcomes of the activities;
- who did what;
- how the resources were used;
- the logistics;
- the time-frame; and
- the relationship between those undertaking the work.

All these minor objectives should lead towards conclusions and recommendations on how to improve the preventive work – the whole point of the evaluation.

The following brief scheme – which can be seen as a model for structuring any planning process – can facilitate evaluation planning. Each section is self-contained and should be included in the evaluation, while the subsections give brief commentaries on how to tackle the subject.

Background study

A background study clarifies the initial situation and positions of the main actors. In any evaluation, it is first important to know where the proposal for the intervention originated and what was identified as the problem. Drug use, after all, is rarely caused by a single factor. The interaction of various elements is the key to understanding drug use. Thus the evaluator should attempt to find out which factors were identified and where the priority lay – not forgetting where the priority did not lie.

The problem looks different from the perspective of a teenager, a social worker or a politician. It is essential, therefore, for the evaluator to identify the individual or organisation that took the lead in defining the phenomenon. It is also important to assess whether all the parties to an intervention agree that it is necessary. A common mistake is for organisations to agree to an intervention that they are not happy with simply as a means of accessing funds. Semantic problems may also arise, with different parties understanding certain key terms, theories and processes in different ways.

Finally, it is important to know whether which methodology to use was discussed. This may seem supplementary, but it is of interest if the intervention is to be evaluated seriously. Knowing why one method was chosen instead of another can be of great value when preparing to analyse the data collected. It also allows external factors which may have favoured one methodology over another to be examined.

Objective study

Studying the intervention's objectives can help in understanding its expected effects. It is essential to consider how the intervention's aims will affect the identified problem. Often, rather than a problem being recognised, solutions are proposed that do not correspond to the problem. If the methodology has been adequately assessed, this pitfall can be avoided.

Just as vital as agreement between all parties about the need for the intervention is agreement as to its objectives and their interpretation.

Methodological study

This element of evaluation investigates whether the methods used for the intervention were appropriate, and asks whether the phenomenon actually 'selected' them, or whether other motives influenced the choice of methodology. The relevance of the methodology should also be discussed with reference to the background study, to see whether the issue was fully explored at this earlier stage.

Process study

Evaluating the process clarifies the interaction between the parties involved which will be useful at later stages. Whether and how the target group was included in planning, executing and evaluating is crucial for the intervention's integrity, and the same questions can be asked of all the parties. Whether the participants were qualified to fulfil their roles with any enthusiasm should also be addressed here.

As for allocating responsibility, the initiating organisation is often responsible for the programme, even if others carry out the work. This normally gives the executive organisation the right to include or exclude others. Thus, analysing the roles of the actors involved can be crucial if the intervention is to be understood. Closely allied to the issue of responsibility is 'communication'. This is not just a technical issue, but rather a description of who made the decisions during the intervention and how these were discussed with the other actors.

Resource study

Resources are always of interest when input is measured alongside outcome. Moreover, the use of resources can say much about why an intervention was successful or not. Conventional issues of income and expenditure obviously need to be addressed. But this is also the point at which to discuss how any financial or resource decisions affected the intervention. For any evaluation, the use to which resources – both human and financial – are put is essential.

Involving the main parties

All the areas mentioned above can be addressed by any evaluation. Some are more difficult than others, but they can all be evaluated. Once this is done, the data can be easily analysed, conclusions reached and recommendations made.

The above list is not only a tool for planning, but also a tool for co-operation and involvement. At each stage, different interpretations will naturally arise which may lead different parties to different conclusions. Conflict can, however, be avoided by involving the main participants in the intervention's planning and implementation. At least three actors should always be involved here: the final target group; the executive organisation; and the funding body.

Ideally, of course, all the relevant actors would be involved in planning the evaluation. But if, for instance, the intervention is a public-information campaign, it may be difficult to engage the target group and this may ultimately be of little importance for the outcome. If, however, the intervention relies on community participation, leaving out the target group is hardly a sensible strategy.

The executive organisation must be involved, and the funding body can choose to be if it so wishes. But even if the funders decide not to participate directly, they should be regularly updated about the evaluation's planning and execution.

An evaluation should satisfy all the main actors, although they will certainly have different opinions about the intervention's outcome. The final target group may ask, 'was the effort any good for me?'; the executive organisation, 'did we do what we promised?'; and the funders, 'did we get what we paid for?' The evaluator's task is to bring these perspectives together and to make them acceptable to all parties.

Terms of reference

The first stage is to draw up agreed 'Terms of Reference' for the work. Such a protocol should ideally contain:

- a background summary of the intervention's history and the aims of the evaluation;
- information on the evaluation's objectives, which must include the main goal as well as supplementary ones, and should be easy to understand;
- a description of the methods to be used in the evaluation;
- an explanation of the different responsibilities of those involved in the evaluation;
- a timetable; and
- an outline of how the information will be reported back (for example, interim reports, the structure of the final report, and so on).

Once all these issues have been settled, the final evaluation is more likely to be accepted and its conclusions and recommendations are more likely to be of real value in the future.

An even stronger way to reinforce the relationship between the evaluator and those who are being evaluated is to set up an evaluation team. The advantage of such a team is that it performs both an internal and external evaluation at the same time. Such a combination of broad knowledge and objectivity (the external evaluator should still maintain control over the final report) makes it much easier for the evaluation to be accepted both within and outside the programme. The negative aspect of evaluation teams is their cost.

What is needed for evaluation

Information on the work undertaken

Reports on the intervention itself can be addressed to various target groups, such as funders, intermediate and final target groups. It is worth comparing these reports to ensure their compatibility.

Data are also vital not only to the original budget and the financial outcome, but also to how the funding situation changed during the course of the intervention. It is very important to analyse whether the financial situation had any impact on the work and its outcome.

Other information relating to the intervention's implementation may include contracts with outside experts, records from decision-making meetings, and other examinations carried out during the intervention (for instance, by a student writing a thesis on the project, or the report of an individual on work placement).

The people involved

Staff members should be interviewed about the intervention and the final target group analysed. Any other groups involved during the planning and implementation stages (such as reference groups, expert witnesses, and so on) should also be asked about their roles in, and impressions of, the programme.

Media interest

It is also useful to evaluate any media coverage the intervention may have received, either locally or nationally. If anything has been written about the programme – either in a book, scientific journal or newspaper – or anything reported by the media, then it should be examined. Such inputs may actually shed new light on the intervention by highlighting any controversial aspects.

Conclusions

This chapter has demonstrated that planning any evaluation involves designing appropriate methods, and preparing for the final report to be accepted.

If evaluation is seen as a tool to improve and develop future preventive work, then it is essential to ensure that people accept it and take notice of its recommendations. If not, the evaluation report – however methodologically sound – will never be used.

Such a situation must be avoided or, at least, the risk of such an outcome minimised by involving the main actors in planning, and even executing, the evaluation. In other words, evaluation requires public relations and communication skills just as much as it requires scientific knowledge.

CHAPTER 6

MEASURING OUTCOMES: METHODOLOGY, THEORY AND MEDIATING VARIABLES

Han Kuipers

The social-science discipline of 'evaluation' first emerged in the 1960s. During the following two decades – especially in the United States – it almost became an industry. But throughout that first boom, evaluation was essentially a non-theoretical, method-driven 'science'. Even highly respected evaluation researchers like Scriven (1967) and Suchman (1967) defined their field in non-theoretical terms. Within this framework, however, competition was fierce between those who had opted for the experimental approach (Cook and Campbell, 1979) and those who defended the naturalistic approach (Guba and Lincoln, 1981).

Developing methodology

In classical experimental designs, the 'experiment' (or intervention) was manipulated in a controlled setting in which subjects were randomly assigned to both experimental and control groups, measurements were objective, and analysis was undertaken using proven statistical techniques. By contrast, the qualitative and ethnographic methods of the naturalistic approach used trained observers to study behaviour in natural settings. Data were analysed using a specific protocol that enabled researchers to interpret the results and formulate concrete conclusions and recommendations.

These differing perspectives on evaluation made valuable contributions to the development of the field. The intensive debate between researchers helped to form a large body of knowledge, so that today an established set of instruments, techniques and procedures is always applied to an evaluation study, while issues such as internal validity and bias are no longer real debating points. The naturalistic approach, with its qualitative methods, has likewise increased awareness of the importance of social context and has provided valid instruments to measure its influence.

The problem, of course, is that experimental designs are inadequate for evaluating a broad-based or fluid programme. In such a case, Weiss and Rein (1969) have stated that the results may be misleading or even artificial. Cronbach (1982) believes that evaluations that follow an experimental design are not very useful for policy decisions because too much attention is paid to trivial issues. That is clearly a serious problem, since most evaluation exists to provide policy-makers with relevant feedback. This has been noted by Chelismky (1977), who reported that programme-stakeholders believe that most evaluations fail to provide them with relevant and useful information. This failure is a result not just of using the experimental design, but also of the evaluator's inadequate understanding of the problem.

Similar difficulties occur with naturalistic methods. Such methods have failed to demonstrate clearly that they generate valid and important information that can be generalised from the specific to the universal (Chen *et al.*, 1988).

As awareness of the deficiencies of traditional approaches has grown, there has been a shift towards combining qualitative and quantitative methods. Although it is clear that doing so will be expensive and requires a combination of skills, the benefits arguably outweigh the costs (Smith, 1986). Smith also proposes that a combined approach is preferable when:

* a complete description is necessary;
* circumstances indicate that the results of a qualitative study can be generalised;
* a combination of methods might enhance validity; and
* qualitative feedback can influence a stakeholder's opinions.

Shotland and Mark (1987), however, point out that an evaluation may be more difficult to interpret when the different methods used generate conflicting results.

Theory development

One result of this focus on research methods has been to neglect theory development for many years. This omission, however, was rectified somewhat in the 1980s with a move towards theory-oriented evaluation. This shift has accelerated in the last few years, for a number of reasons. First, too many interventions were classified as ineffective because the focus on methodology meant that a programme's effectiveness was often left unaddressed. Second, it was believed that evaluation as a discipline needed its own theory. Third, closer attention began to be paid to the format and content of an intervention. Finally, researchers began to believe that methods should be considered as the means to develop knowledge and not as its end.

The traditional method-oriented approach can be seen as a 'black-box' form of evaluation. It is a rather simple input–output model which seems not to acknowledge any of the complexity of the social process that takes place when any system is exposed to an intervention. Lipsey (1987) urges the development of a theoretical framework to differentiate the causal processes that serve as a basis for planning and organising evaluation activities. It has also been proposed (Cordray, 1986) that evaluation should broaden the evidential basis by actively considering plausible alternative explanations, by examining implementation procedures and by investigating mediating and contextual factors.

This shift towards theory-driven evaluation does not, by any means, herald the rejection of appropriate research methods. What it does mean, however, is that the theory-driven perspective, although developed as a reaction against the traditional 'black-box' approach, has to be seen as an expansion of traditional perspectives (Chen, 1990).

Theory-driven evaluation and drug prevention

A number of intervention examples have been developed within the field of primary prevention in line with this perspective. The most common is the use of a theoretical framework known as 'social influences'.

The 'social-influences' approach is premised on the fact that actors in the social environment (parents, peers and the media) can exert great influence – either positively or negatively – on young people's risk-taking behaviour. Youngsters should therefore be taught and trained to strengthen non-risk-taking behaviour and to transform their risk-taking into non-risk-taking behaviour. They must be equipped to identify social pressure both from their peers and from their families, and they must be taught the skills to resist these pressures. This 'social-influences' approach is broadly based on three theoretical models: Social Learning Theory (Bandura, 1977); Problem Behaviour Theory (Jessor, 1987); and the Theory of Reasoned Action (Ajzen and Fishbein, 1980).

Mediating variables

These theories provide a framework in which to understand individual and group health behaviour and to prevent health problems (Flay and Petraitis, 1991; Lorion *et al.*, 1989). Social Learning Theory's concept of 'modelling' is a case in point – non-smoking parents can be a positive model for their children in terms of smoking behaviour. Such a concept can act as a 'mediating variable' within a prevention intervention, a variable which has been defined thus:

> A variable functions as a mediator if the variable accounts for the relation between exposure to the prevention program and the outcome measure.
> (Baron and Kenny, 1986)

In other words, a theoretical basis can be constructed for choosing the mediating variable. The intervention is set up and tested in a way that ensures it will influence this mediating variable and consequently affect the outcome.

Mediator analysis

In the context of theory-driven evaluation, a prevention programme can be said to be designed to change mediating variables that are assumed to be causally related to outcome. If this causal relationship is proven, and if it is also proven that the intervention affects the mediating variables, then, all being equal, the prevention programme will change the outcome (MacKinnon, 1994).

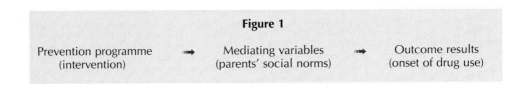

Figure 1

Prevention programme ➡ Mediating variables ➡ Outcome results
(intervention)   (parents' social norms)   (onset of drug use)

Mediating variables can be biological, psychological or behavioural. As discussed above, drug-prevention programmes based on the social-influences approach have to be designed to increase resistance skills or to establish conservative norms towards drug use (Flay, 1985).

Mediator analysis (MacKinnon, 1994) is based on the effect an independent variable such as exposure to drugs can have on mediating variables, and the link between programme effects on mediating variables and programme effects on outcome.

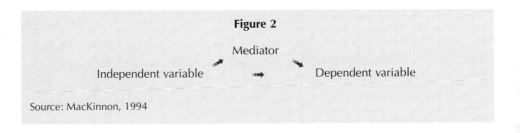

Figure 2

Mediator

Independent variable ➡ Dependent variable

Source: MacKinnon, 1994

By measuring mediating variables, researchers gain not only vital information about the prevention intervention, but also increase their knowledge of the theoretical model that acts as the intervention's framework. Such an analysis is variously known as 'process analysis' (Baron and Kenny, 1986) or 'effect decomposition' (Hayduk, 1987). Neither term is really suitable, however, as the former also refers to evaluating the implementation process and the latter is commonly used in non-experimental studies to distinguish between the direct and indirect effects of an independent variable on outcome. That is why this author prefers the term 'mediator analysis' as introduced by MacKinnon.

Mediator analysis is necessary for several reasons. MacKinnon (1994) lists the most important ones:

- It provides a check on whether the intervention had the desired effects on the mediating variables.
- It identifies successful and unsuccessful components of an intervention and enables those who developed it to improve on it.
- It provides information about how the intervention achieved its effects and generates more data on underlying mechanisms and processes.
- It tests the theoretical assumptions of the model on which the prevention intervention is based.

Looking more closely at the statistical analysis of mediating variables, it is clear that, in practice, interventions target a great many mediators and that achieving a completely random selection of subjects is not easy. But even when such a selection is possible, it is still difficult to interpret the relationship between mediator and outcome. If, for instance, it is felt that an intervention has no effect, rather than jettisoning the entire programme, as has so often happened in the past, mediator analysis could provide a more useful interpretation of the reasons for failure. It could be argued that individual mediators have some effect (whether positive or negative), but that, taken as a whole, they cancel each other out.

The effect of a mediator on an outcome must, of course, be statistically significant. If not, the only evidence is that an assumed relationship between mediating variable and health behaviour is unproven. Even then, such an apparently inconclusive result can still contribute to the development of theory because it questions a theoretical assumption which may, on closer inspection, have no basis in fact.

Methodological problems

No research methodology is perfect. Often, there is not enough time to be totally thorough (in undertaking the literature study, planning, piloting, making adjustments and implementation), affecting the degree to which internal and external validity can be guaranteed. Evaluators and stakeholders must be aware of these possible shortcomings.

Another aspect is the paradoxical effect that an innovative and radical intervention may have on its own outcome. Sometimes an intervention is just too 'interesting' and attracts a much larger target group than it can cope with. Such effects can, however, end up as mediating variables (media attention, for instance, can reinforce a desired outcome). But whatever the case, these effects force the evaluator to state very clearly how the results are to be interpreted.

Examples of evaluation studies

Hansen *et al.* (1988) conducted an evaluation study in which the effects of three alcohol-prevention curricula on a number of hypothesised mediating variables were tested and compared. The three curricula were based on different mediating concepts all derived from the 'social-influences' approach: teaching social resistance skills; strengthening conservative norms towards drinking; and increasing understanding of the consequences of alcohol consumption. The results confirm that the curricula did affect the mediators and the outcome. In other words, the study adds to the evidence that there is a relationship between the mediating variables and the targeted behaviour. Furthermore, it demonstrates that the constructed interventions have proved effective.

Gorman (1992) reviews a number of evaluation studies to understand more about the use of theory in developing interventions. The prevention projects reviewed – Project SMART (Self-Management and Resistance Training), Project ALERT, the Life Skills Training (LST) Programme and the Midwestern Prevention Programme (MPP) – were also developed from the social-influences model, but their results illustrate that no single prevention strategy is universally effective. Gorman argues that this suggests that a comprehensive prevention strategy is not viable and that interventions should be more specifically targeted at, for example, non-users, experimental users or regular users. In addition, the more that is known about mediating concepts the better able researchers will be to tailor prevention to specific groups and specific health behaviours.

Ellickson *et al.* (1993) examined the impact of Project ALERT on a number of mediating variables believed to affect actual drug use. These variables included adolescents' beliefs in their ability to resist drugs, what they perceive as the consequences of drug use, their perceptions of peer use, and their tolerance to drugs and expectations of further use. A survey of 4,000 US seventh and eighth graders revealed that the programme affected perceptions about the use of tobacco, alcohol and cannabis. It showed that the curriculum successfully reduced cognitive risk factors, indicating that the social-influence model can have an impact on a broad range of drug-related beliefs.

The final example is again provided by Hansen (1996). A new prevention intervention was tested in a recently published pilot study. The mediating variables were: a personal commitment to avoid participating in high-risk behaviour; ideals that conflicted with high-risk behaviour; bonding with 'pro-social' institutions; and conventional beliefs about social norms. The study's primary purpose was to evaluate the programme's potential to change variables that had been identified by empirical research as strong mediators for initial substance use. The conclusion was that the programme successfully changed the targeted variables which in turn are heavily correlated to the targeted behaviours.

Conclusion

This chapter has demonstrated that prevention programmes should be based on theoretical models. This is because theories can help to target mediating variables, which should be chosen in accordance with empirical findings. In turn, mediator analysis can help to interpret the outcome and improve the intervention.

MacKinnon (1994) states that mediator analysis is rarely conducted. Perhaps this will change in the near future as more researchers become accustomed to analysing the results of theory-driven evaluation. Hansen argues that recent developments make it possible (and also vital) to conduct studies that treat mediating variables as an integral part of programme development and evaluation. His own study (Hansen, 1996) must be considered as the first example – although hopefully not the last – of the possibilities that mediator analysis offers for the future.

References

Ajzen, I., and Fishbein, M. (1980) *Understanding Attitudes and Predictive Social Behaviour,* Englewood Cliffs, NJ: Prentice Hall.

Bandura, A. (1977) *Social Learning Theory*, Englewood Cliffs, NJ: Prentice Hall.

Baron, R., and Kenny, D. (1986) 'The moderator–mediator variable distinction in social-psychological research: Conceptual, strategic and statistical considerations', *Journal of Personality and Social Psychology*, 51(6) , 1173–1182.

Chelismky, E. (1977) *A Symposium on the Use of Evaluations by Federal Agencies*, Vol. 1, McLean, VA: Mitre Corporation.

Chen, H. (1990) *Theory-driven Evaluations*, Newbury Park, CA: Sage.

Chen, H., *et al.* (1988) 'Evaluating an antismoking program: diagnostics of underlying causal mechanisms', *Evaluation and the Health Professions*, 11(4), 441–464.

Cook, T., and Campbell, D. (1979) *Quasi-experimentation*, Chicago, IL: Rand McNally.

Cordray, D. (1986) 'Quasi-experimental analysis: a mixture of methods and judgment', in Trochim, W. (Ed.) *Advances in Quasi-experimental Design and Analysis. New Directions for Program Evaluation*, San Francisco, CA: Jossey-Bass.

Cronbach, L. (1982) *Designing Evaluations of Educational and Social Programs*, San Francisco, CA: Jossey-Bass.

Ellickson, P., *et al.* (1993) 'Changing adolescent propensities to use drugs: results from project ALERT', *Health Education Quarterly*, 20(2), 227–242.

Flay, B. (1985) 'Psychosocial approaches to smoking prevention: A review of findings', *Health Psychology*, 4(5), 449–488.

Flay, B., and Petraitis, J. (1991) 'Methodological issues in drug use prevention research: theoretical foundations', in Leukefeld, S., and Bukoski, W. (Eds) *Drug Prevention Intervention Research: Methodological Issues*, Rockville, MD: National Institute on Drug Abuse (NIDA).

Gorman, D. (1992) 'Using theory and basic research to target primary prevention programs: recent developments and future prospects', *Alcohol and Alcoholism*, 27(6), 583–594.

Guba, E., and Lincoln, Y. (1981) *Effective Evaluation: Improving the Usefulness of Evaluation Results Through Responsive and Naturalistic Approaches*, San Francisco, CA: Jossey-Bass.

Hansen, W. (1996) 'Pilot test results comparing the All Stars program with seventh grade DARE: program integrity and mediating variable analysis', *Substance Use and Misuse*, 33(10), 1359–1377.

Hansen, W., *et al.* (1988). 'Differential impact of three alcohol prevention curricula on hypothesized mediating variables', *Journal of Drug Education*, 18(2), 143–154.

Hayduk, L. (1987) *Structural Equation Modeling with LISREL: Essentials and Advances*, Baltimore, MD: Johns Hopkins University Press.

Jessor, R. (1987) 'Problem-behaviour theory, psychosocial development, and adolescent problem drinking', *Journal of Addiction*, 82(4), 331–342.

Lipsey, M. (1987) 'Theory as method: small theories of treatments', Paper presented to the National Center for Health Services Research Conference, 'Strengthening Causal Interpretations of Non-experimental Data', Tucson, AZ.

Lorion, R., *et al.* (1989) 'The prevention of child and adolescent disorders: from theory to research', in Shaffer, D., *et al.* (Eds) *Prevention of Mental Disorders, Alcohol and Other Drug Use in Children and Adolescents,* Office for Substance Abuse Prevention Monograph 2, Washington DC: US Government Printing Office.

MacKinnon, D. (1994) 'Analysis of mediating variables in prevention and intervention research', in Cázares, A., and Beatty, L. (Eds) *Scientific Methods for Prevention Intervention Research,* Rockville, MD: NIDA.

Scriven, M. (1967) 'The methodology of evaluation', in R. E. Stake *et al.* (Eds) *Perspectives on Curriculum Evaluation,* Chicago, IL: Rand McNally.

Shotland, R., and Mark, M. (1987) 'Improving inferences from multiple methods', in Mark and Shotland (Eds) *Multiple Methods in Program Evaluation. New Directions for Program Evaluation,* San Francisco, CA: Jossey-Bass.

Smith, M. (1986) 'The whole is greater: combining qualitative and quantitative approaches in evaluation studies', in Williams, D. (Ed.) *Naturalistic Evaluation. New Directions for Program Evaluations,* San Francisco, CA: Jossey-Bass.

Suchman, E. (1967) *Evaluation Research,* New York: Russell Sage.

Weiss, R., and Rein, M. (1969) 'The evaluation of broad-aim programs: a cautionary case and moral', *Annals of the American Academy of Political and Social Science,* 385(1), 133–142.

CHAPTER 7

INSTRUMENTS AND MEASUREMENT IN EVALUATION STUDIES

Mark Morgan

Evaluating programmes designed to prevent the onset of drug use has produced mixed results (Tobler, 1986; Moskowitz, 1989; Morgan, forthcoming). Therefore, the care and attention that developing and applying evaluative measures require cannot be overstressed. Appropriate evaluative instruments not only indicate whether or not an intervention was successful (summative evaluation), but they can also inform the success of a programme's implementation (formative evaluation) as well as the ways in which outcomes are approached.

Reliability and validity

The extent to which measuring instruments, and questionnaires in particular, are a reliable and valid indicator of substance misuse is central to all evaluation. In general, recent evidence supports the conclusions of earlier work that indicate that questionnaires fare well when compared to other tools, such as physiological measures or collateral reports on 'significant others' (Akers *et al.*, 1983). Nor is there much evidence to suggest that additional techniques enhance the validity of a questionnaire above and beyond that which is obtained under conditions of anonymity and confidentiality (Evans *et al.*, 1977).

However, while accepting that self-report items are in principle the most effective way to gather evaluation information, not all questionnaire designs are equally trustworthy. Two of the more salient features that can affect validity and reliability were isolated in a study by Embree and Whitehead (1993). These features are a question's capacity to aid recall, and the extent to which a question prompts a socially desirable response. Questions that produce valid and reliable responses, the researchers concluded, do so for identifiable reasons, and measurement instruments can be radically improved by assimilating these particular features.

Studies of internal reliability demonstrate that questions are notoriously sensitive to wording. A UK study (Measham *et al.*, 1994) found that 27% of 14–15-year-olds replied to questions inconsistently, stating that they had tried cannabis in the last year and then contradicting this in a later answer. It should be noted, however, that there was a subtle difference between the questions: the first one referred to *trying* cannabis; the later one to *smoking* the drug. But whatever the reason for this inconsistency, phrasing is clearly crucial.

Measurement issues in evaluation

Table 1 below illustrates the measurement questions used in some recent evaluation studies.

Table 1: Evaluation studies

Study/Country	Focus	Measures
Ellickson *et al.* (1993) *US high school*	Project ALERT versus control groups	Range of risk factors including beliefs, attitudes and skills
Donaldson *et al.* (1994) *US fifth grade*	Evaluation of Project Alcohol and Drug Use (ADU)	Resistance skills, perception of norms
Botvin *et al.* (1995a) *US high school*	Comparison of prevention with control group	Self-reports for legal and illegal substances
Botvin *et al.* (1995b) *US high school*	At-risk minority students targeted with culturally appropriate programme	Self-reports and intentions of legal and illegal drug use
Gislason *et al.* (1995) *Iceland*	Skills for Adolescence (SFA) programme versus control groups	Self-reports of prevalence
Dukes *et al.* (1996) *US high school*	DARE programme versus control groups	Self-reports of legal and illegal drug use: resistance to peer pressure, self-esteem
Emshoff *et al.* (1996) *US parents and children*	Evaluation of programme designed to enhance self- and cultural esteem	Outcomes confined to measuring 'mediating' influences
Gottfredson *et al.* (1996) *US high school*	Evaluation of programme targeting school curriculum and norms	Outcomes include unobtrusive school measures (attendance and suspensions)
Morgan *et al.* (1996) *Ireland, 14–16-year-olds*	Comparison of 'On My Own Two Feet' programme with control group	Self-reports of legal and illegal substances: beliefs, attitudes and intentions

A number of features emerge. First, it can be seen that self-report questionnaires are the dominant measurement instrument. While there are clearly other approaches, as in the unobtrusive measures reported by Gottfredson *et al.* (1996), these tend to be used as supplementary data to back up the questionnaires.

Second, most of the studies did not focus exclusively on illegal substances, but tended also to be concerned with legal substances, especially alcohol. In some instances, this resulted in an index of substance misuse that combined alcohol with other drugs. It is also worth noting that, in most cases, 'classical' prevalence terms were employed, such as lifetime use of a substance, use in the previous 12 months and use in the previous 30 days. This usually involved some measure of frequency for those respondents who answered positively.

Third, in most cases the measurement tools were specifically created for the study in question. This has a number of negative consequences. It makes comparisons between studies difficult, and questions the validity of the specific instruments that have typically been designed for that particular evaluation.

A fourth point is that 'mediating variables' were used in some studies to assess factors other than purely drug-related outcomes (see Chapter 6 for more on mediator analysis). In some cases, these mediating variables were cognitive or attitudinal (for example, attitudes towards drug use or developing resistance skills), while in others – for example, self-esteem – they were less directly related to behaviour. What these variables have in common, however, is that although they are not solely related to drug use, they are assumed on the basis of theoretical models of behavioural change to exert some influence on drug use.

Finally, relatively few of the studies in Table 1 appeared to be concerned with programme implementation. Thus, when results were not as predicted, it is unclear whether this was due to non-adherence to the programme. This issue is extremely important, as failure needs to be explained, if only to avoid the same mistakes in future. The relationship between programme adherence and outcome has been demonstrated by Pentz *et al.* (1990), who evaluated this relationship in the US Midwestern Prevention Project (MPP). Implementation was measured through teacher self-reports and by research-staff reports. Drug use was measured by student self-reports and a breathalyser was used to verify the accuracy of self-reported drug use. It was found that levels of implementation were strongly related to outcome.

Table 2 overleaf gives a brief but instructive comparison of the evaluation studies covered in Table 1. It examines a small sample of recent studies that were not concerned with evaluation, but with causal and mediating factors. What is perhaps most striking is that the measures used in these latter studies bear a remarkable resemblance to those employed by the evaluation studies. As in Table 1, the basic measure is that of prevalence, while the studies in Table 2 typically targeted other mediating factors believed to influence behaviour.

Table 2: Studies of causal and mediating factors

Study/Country	Focus	Measures
Morgan and Grube (1991) *Ireland 13–17-year-olds*	Peer influences on drug use	Prevalence and frequency measures; peer approval and peer behaviour
Measham *et al.* (1994) *England 14–15-year-olds*	'Normalisation' of drug use	Prevalence measures as well as 'offer' questions
Jessor *et al.* (1995) *US seventh to ninth grade*	Risk and protective factors in problem behaviour	Drug use as a problem behaviour, measures of protective factors
McCusker *et al.* (1995) *Welsh adolescents*	Conceptual basis for different forms of usage	On basis of prevalence and intention, four categories of user defined
Kandel and Davies (1996) *US high school*	Profile of six stages of drug use, legal and illegal	Prevalence measures of legal and illegal drugs
Wills and Cleary (1996) *US seventh to ninth grade*	Mediating factors in legal and illegal drug use	Measures of peer influence

Current developments

Models of drug use

Most measurement procedures are not based on a particular 'model' of substance misuse. Instead, they tend to use simple prevalence measures and, in some cases, a concept of what is meant by 'misuse' is introduced to the study after the event. In other words, rather than deciding on an *a priori* basis that particular levels of substance use constitute a 'problem', categories of use are formed on the basis of information extracted from questionnaires. Normally, these categories are based on 'frequency of use', but sometimes other measures are introduced, such as the number of substances used, the use of legal substances and the context of their use.

For instance, in the McCusker *et al.* study (1995), respondents were divided into one of four groups based on their responses to specific questions about past use and future intentions. These groups could then be differentiated from one another in terms of social and personal factors. The resistant group was made up of those who had never taken any of the illegal drugs and who said that they would definitely refuse them if offered. The vulnerable group were those who, although they had never tried a drug, would either take one if offered or were not sure if they would do so. The experimental group was defined as those who had used an illegal drug but only 'once or twice', whereas the repeated user group were those who continued to use illegal substances either 'sometimes' or 'regularly'.

Such efforts to conceptualise drug use are valuable, but only when their construct validity can be sustained (that is, when the distinctions between types of use and users can be supported in terms of influences and consequences). Because of this, evidence that consistently supports any particular conceptualisation is scarce. A standard example of an evaluation that ensured construct validity is the Shedler and Block (1990) study that contrasted discrete groups of non-users, experimenters and abusers. The main measure of personality characteristics was the California Q-sort made up of 100 personality descriptive statements from which a profile can be extracted. These measures were obtained at the same time as, but independently of, the measures of substance use. In addition, psychological descriptions were available for all the subjects from early childhood onwards.

The results indicated that adolescents who had experimented with drugs (primarily with cannabis) were the 'best' adjusted of the sample. In contrast, those who used drugs frequently were maladjusted, with a distinct personality syndrome marked by alienation, poor impulse control and manifest emotional distress. Finally, those who had never experimented with any drug by the age of 18 were relatively anxious, emotionally constricted and lacking in social skills.

Broadening the basis of prevention efforts

Another feature of recent studies is that the interventions tend to have a broader community base, frequently involving parents, churches, community groups, the local media as well as schools (see, for example, Pentz et al., 1990; Johnson et al., 1996; LoSciuto et al., 1996). In some cases, targeting a particular community has led to a programme being modified to ensure that it is culturally appropriate. This was the case in the study carried out by Botvin et al. (1995b) which compared the effectiveness of a prevention programme based on generic skills with a 'culturally modified' one. The results suggested that the latter programme was more effective in terms of substance use and future intentions.

While the move to broader community-based projects is laudable given the limited success of projects with a narrower focus, it does mean that efforts to gauge the impact of the intervention can be hampered. If, for instance, posters, magazines and leaflets are distributed widely throughout a community, measuring the effects of these media is more difficult than if only one leaflet had been distributed in one school. Furthermore, it is almost impossible to isolate the precise factors responsible for observed outcomes.

This broadening of prevention efforts also targets other behavioural variables. In line with the stance taken by Jessor et al. (1995) that drug use is just one aspect of a larger syndrome of 'problem behaviour', some studies have sought to change antisocial behaviour itself. Thus, the task of measuring outcomes has spiralled to include issues such as delinquency, precocious sexual activity, rebelliousness and truancy.

Targeting risk factors

Targeting students identified as being 'at risk' is yet another recent development (see, for example, Gottfredson *et al.*, 1996; Richards-Colocino *et al.*, 1996). One of the problems with this approach, as with broadening the effort, is that it involves myriad potential factors, most of which are not easily susceptible to simple targeting. Researchers can also be 'duped' by deceptively obvious factors, such as social background, which have not been shown in the international literature to have a strong relationship with drug use.

The risk-focused approach has been advocated largely because of the success of campaigns aimed at reducing risk factors for coronary heart disease. Proponents of this approach have pointed to the failure of campaigns that ignored risk factors, and while 'risk' is a valid variable, Hawkins *et al.* (1992) have demonstrated that a number of steps must be taken if the approach is to demonstrate its worth: high-risk factors need to be identified for substance use; effective strategies for reducing such risks must also be identified; and these methods must then be applied, both to high-risk and to general populations. It is fair to say that very few studies have actually managed to carry through all three steps. From the point of view of measurement, a crucial ingredient that is all-too-often missing from the risk-focused approach is measuring changes in the risk factor being targeted.

Lessons from negative outcomes

In examining the many studies of prevention programmes that have been carried out, the relatively small impact evaluation has had on practice is striking. There is little evidence that programmes that have produced negative results have been discarded in favour of more promising programmes, or even that the lessons from negative results have been learnt. For example, as stated earlier, it is now becoming increasingly clear that a major factor in negative results is the failure to implement the programme properly. A recent evaluation found this to be extremely significant. Students were divided into those who had experienced the full programme, and those who had only partially experienced it, and dramatic differences were found (Botvin *et al.*, 1995a).

It also appears that the efficacy of a programme is only one, and perhaps not even the most important, factor in determining whether a particular prevention approach is adopted. It seems that the 'face validity' of a programme may be especially influential in convincing policy-makers and educators of its effectiveness. If an approach appears to 'tell it as it is' about drugs, then, regardless of the results of formal evaluations, an objective view might suggest that the approach will work. But whatever the reason, evaluations are only one factor in deciding the fate of a programme.

Conclusion

This chapter has demonstrated that using structured questionnaires is one of the best ways to measure evaluation outcomes. Currently, most measurement approaches are very similar to those in the fields of epidemiology and causal analysis. But less attention has been paid to the distinctive aspects of evaluation itself, such as effective implementation and the extent to which participants experience all the aspects of a programme. The challenges which these and other issues pose for evaluation cannot be avoided.

Acknowledgements

Thanks are due to Joel Grube, Prevention Research Center, Berkeley, CA, for his assistance with the work that formed the background to this chapter.

References

Akers, R., et al. (1983) 'Are self-reports of adolescent deviant behaviour valid? Biochemical measures, randomised response and the bogus pipeline technique', Social Forces, 62, 234–251.

Botvin, G., et al. (1995a) 'Long-term follow-up results of a randomized drug abuse prevention trial in a white middle class population', Journal of the American Medical Association, 273(14), 1106–1112.

Botvin, G., et al. (1995b) 'Effects of culturally focused and generic skills training approaches to alcohol and drug abuse prevention among minority adolescents: two-year follow-up results', Psychology of Addictive Behaviors, 9, 183–194.

Donaldson, S., et al. (1994) 'Testing the generalizability of intervening mechanism theories: understanding the effects of adolescent drug use prevention interventions', Journal of Behavioral Medicine, 17(2), 195–216.

Dukes, R., et al. (1996) 'Three year follow-up of drug abuse resistance (DARE)', Evaluation Review, 20, 49–66.

Ellickson, P., et al. (1993) 'Preventing adolescent drug use: long-term results of a junior high program', American Journal of Public Health, 83(6), 856–861.

Embree, B., and Whitehead, P. (1993) 'Validity and reliability of self-reported drinking behavior: dealing with the problem of response bias', Journal of Studies on Alcohol, 54(3), 334–344.

Emshoff, J., et al. (1996) 'Findings from SUPERSTARS: a health promotion program for families to enhance multiple protective factors', Journal of Adolescent Research, 11, 68–96.

Evans, R., et al. (1977) 'Increasing the validity of self-reports of smoking behaviour in children', Journal of Applied Psychology, 62(4), 521–523.

Gislason, T., et al. (1995) 'Alcohol consumption, smoking and drug use among Icelandic teenagers: a study into the effectiveness of the Skills for Adolescence Programme, Drugs: Education, Prevention and Policy, 2, 243–258.

Gottfredson, D., *et al.* (1996) 'A multimodel school-based prevention program', *Journal of Adolescent Research*, 11, 97–115.

Hawkins, J., *et al.* (1992) 'Risk and protective factors for alcohol and other drug problems in adolescence and early adulthood: implications for substance abuse prevention', *Psychological Bulletin*, 112(1), 64–105.

Jessor, R., *et al.* (1995) 'Protective factors in adolescent problem behaviour: moderator effects and developmental change', *Developmental Psychology*, 31, 923–933.

Johnson, K., *et al.* (1996) 'Reducing alcohol and other drug use by strengthening community, family, and youth resilience: evaluation of the Creating Lasting Connections program', *Journal of Adolescent Research*, 11, 36–67.

Kandel, D., and Davies, M. (1996) 'High school students who use crack and other drugs', *Archives for General Psychiatry*, 53(1), 71–80.

LoSciuto, L., *et al.* (1996) 'An outcome evaluation of Across Ages: an intergenerational mentoring approach to drug prevention', *Journal of Adolescent Research*, 11, 116–129.

McCusker, C., *et al.* (1995) 'Teenagers and illicit drug use: expanding the "user vs. non-user" dichotomy', *Journal of Community and Applied Social Psychology*, 5, 221–241.

Measham, F., *et al.* (1994) 'The normalisation of recreational drug use amongst young people in North-West England', *British Journal of Sociology*, 45(2), 287–312.

Morgan, M. (forthcoming) *Evaluations of Substance Use Prevention Programmes: Implications for Illicit Drugs*, COST A-6, Brussels: European Communities.

Morgan, M., and Grube, J. (1991) 'Closeness and peer group influence', *British Journal of Social Psychology*, 30, 159–169.

Morgan, M., *et al.* (1996) 'Prevention of substance misuse: rationale and effectiveness of the programme "On My Own Two Feet"', *OIDEAS: Journal of the Department of Education*, 44, 526.

Moskowitz, J. (1989) 'The primary prevention of alcohol problems: a critical review of the research literature', *Journal of Studies on Alcohol*, 50(1), 54–88.

Pentz, M., *et al.* (1990) 'Effects of program implementation on adolescent drug use behavior: the Midwestern Prevention Project (MPP)', *Evaluation Review*, 14, 264–289.

Richards-Colocino, N., *et al.* (1996) 'Project success: comprehensive intervention services for middle-school high-risk youth', *Journal of Adolescent Research*, 11, 130–163.

Shedler, J., and Block, J. (1990) 'Adolescent drug use and psychological health. A longitudinal inquiry', *American Psychologist*, 45(5), 612–630.

Tobler, N. (1986) 'Meta-analysis of 143 adolescent drug prevention programs: quantitative outcome results of program participants compared to a control or comparison group', *Journal of Drug Issues*, 16, 537–567.

Wills, T., and Cleary, S. (1996) 'How are social support effects mediated? A test with parental support and adolescent substance use', *Journal of Personality and Social Psychology*, 71(5), 937–952.

CHAPTER 8

THE COST-EFFECTIVENESS OF DRUG PREVENTION

Christine Godfrey and Steve Parrott

The resources available globally for drug-prevention initiatives are severely limited and there is often considerable competition for funds. While interest in judging the cost-effectiveness of different prevention initiatives has grown, very few published studies are available – although a number of general guides to economic evaluations do exist (for example, Tolley, 1992; Gold *et al.*, 1996; Drummond *et al.*, 1997). Such economic evaluations are closely linked to outcome-evaluation techniques –– identifying, measuring and then valuing both the outcomes (benefits) and the inputs (costs) of a number of alternative interventions or scenarios. As such, these evaluations mirror many of the disciplines already outlined in previous chapters, and can be just as valuable when gauging the relative success of different prevention approaches.

What questions can economic evaluation address?

At the strategic level, policy-makers use economic evaluation when considering in which areas additional resources would yield more benefits – treatment, prevention or enforcement. Rydell and Everingham (1994) undertook such an analysis of cocaine policies in the United States, and concluded that demand-oriented pro-grammes were much more cost-effective than enforcement activities designed to reduce the supply of drugs. Economic evaluation can help answer other broad questions about budget allocation between settings, population groups, drug types and forms of drug use.

These issues can then be broken down further. In any specific setting, such as a school or workplace, questions may also relate to the balance of resources between primary and secondary prevention. Other economic evaluations may compare different prevention programmes with similar goals – such as public-information campaigns versus venue-specific interventions – while still more specific evaluations would, for example, address the cost-effectiveness of different methods of delivering school-based prevention.

Questions are, however, rarely framed as stark choices between one type of prevention programme and another. More realistically, policy-makers have to choose how to combine different approaches. Often choices are made at a marginal level, determining how to use a small increase in overall resources or planning how resources should be cut. At a more systematic level, questions can be framed to eval-uate adding or removing one element of a more complex programme. Would, for instance, the addition of a mass-media campaign increase the overall effectiveness of a national health programme?

There is, therefore, a very long list of questions that economic-evaluation techniques may help address, and many different reasons for asking them. Policy-makers and funders are likely to be interested in some of the broader issues, while those engaged in providing drug-prevention programmes on the ground may be more interested in the relative value of specific aspects of the programme they are delivering.

Those asking the questions may also determine the study's perspective and, consequently, the types of costs and benefits included and the alternatives to be evaluated. Workplace interventions provide an interesting example of how different perspectives can shape an economic evaluation. Employers are principally interested in the effects of programmes within their workplace. They are concerned with factors such as productivity, sick leave, job turnover and safety. If the study is conducted solely from this perspective, only the costs and benefits that occur in the workplace would be identified, measured and valued. The most cost-effective or cost-beneficial programme from the employers' perspective may not, however, be the most cost-effective from a different perspective. For example, one particular programme may involve referring individuals to community-based rather than in-house workplace services – in other words, shifting the costs. From a society perspective, in-house services may be more cost-effective than the community-based alternative, and there may be more benefit to the community if its services are used for groups other than those employed in a particular workplace. Most economists would therefore suggest that a full societal perspective tracing all costs and benefits – not just current cash flow – is necessary.

Different types of economic evaluation

Economists start from the basic principle that all resources – land, labour, raw materials, capital and human skills – are scarce. Using a particular resource means that the potential benefits associated with putting it to some other purpose are lost. Judging whether a community's scarce resources have been used to maximise the benefits to the citizen is one of the primary criteria for economists. In other words, economists are not only seeking to answer the question 'does a drug-prevention programme work?', but also 'can the resources needed to make the programme work be better used elsewhere?' While this type of efficiency is the economist's main criterion, other goals may also have to be considered. For example, policy-makers may well be concerned about specific groups in society, such as the young and disadvantaged. Thus it may also be important to identify which groups 'gain' from the particular intervention and which groups 'pay' for it.

There are four main types of full economic evaluation:

* cost minimisation;
* cost-effectiveness;
* cost utility; and
* cost–benefit analysis.

Full economic evaluations require examining both costs and benefits, and comparing two of more alternatives. Other types of economic studies attempt to estimate the social costs of drug use, but these are not classed as evaluations as such and are not discussed in this chapter. A full description and guidelines for undertaking such studies are given in Single *et al.* (1996).

Partial economic evaluations can also be undertaken. Some studies examine the resource inputs or costs in more detail, such as the factors that influence the costs of delivering prevention interventions to different groups, or the costs of different components of the intervention. Some health-promotion studies have examined the relationship between outcomes and the resource inputs for one particular type of programme (see Shipley *et al.*, 1995, for an example of this using 'Quit and Win' stopping-smoking competitions).

In all types of economic evaluation, the costs are measured and valued in monetary units. In general, many of the wider benefits of programmes, such as health-care savings or criminal-justice costs, are also measured and valued in money terms. The distinction between the four types of economic evaluation is how to measure and value the narrower benefits for the individuals targeted by the intervention.

Cost minimisation

This form of evaluation tends to assume that the various interventions under consideration are equally effective and that the benefits for the individual are also broadly equivalent. Obviously, if this assumption is made, the analysis only needs to consider the costs of the various interventions. This simplifies the task, but the assumption made is a major one and is unlikely to apply in the real world.

Cost-effectiveness

Cost-effectiveness analysis is the most common economic-evaluation technique. Indeed, the very term 'cost-effectiveness' is often assumed to be generic to all types of economic evaluation. Technically, however, it only refers to those evaluations in which the effects on individuals targeted by the intervention are measured in some 'natural' unit. This unit could be drug prevalence, incidence, problematic drug use, morbidity or mortality. Examples include the proportion of the target group that is drug-free at some given time; the change in overall levels of drug use attributable to the interventions; and changes in different problem indicators, such as needle-sharing, or even quality of life. There are, of course, many other choices for outcome indicators, and this choice depends largely on the purpose of the study. Evaluative studies may adopt a package of outcome measures, but problems can arise if researchers do not follow a pre-arranged analysis plan. There is always a risk that some bias may occur if the indicator is chosen after the evaluation is complete.

Alternative interventions are compared in cost-effectiveness studies either on the basis of the lowest net cost required to achieve some set level of the outcome indicator, or by identifying the intervention with the highest outcome levels for a given budget. The choice of an adequate outcome measure is clearly an important part of this analysis. Net costs are defined as the total costs of the intervention less any non-individual benefits measured in monetary terms. By calculating net costs per unit of outcome across the different alternatives, it can also be determined whether one intervention dominates others in terms of costs and outcomes, whatever the level of target outcome or resources. In addition, any trade-offs in costs and outcomes between the different interventions can be identified. In practice, alternative outcome measures may be presented, especially in an area such as drug prevention where no agreed generic measures are available.

Cost-effectiveness is best suited to situations in which the programmes being compared have very similar goals. It becomes much more difficult to use cost-effectiveness as a tool to compare interventions with different settings or targets. It would, for example, be difficult to isolate one measure that would adequately compare a school-based programme aimed at reducing drug initiation, and a programme for reducing injecting drug use among current drug users.

Cost utility

The other types of economic evaluation use broader outcome measures to ease comparison for interventions that may be competing for scarce resources. Cost-utility analysis uses multiple individual outcome measures to combine an individual's expected lifespan with many of the dimensions that would influence their health-related quality of life. These measures, such as Quality Adjusted Life Years (QALY), have been used in studies of smoking-prevention programmes (Fiscella and Franks, 1996) and HIV-directed measures (Holtgrave and Kelly, 1996). However, as these measures focus only on health-related quality of life, they may be inadequate for capturing all the benefits to an individual of a drug-prevention programme.

Cost–benefit analysis

An alternative measure is to attempt to place a value on the programme for the individual by measuring outcomes in monetary terms. If all costs and consequences – including those to individuals – are measured in money, the economic evaluation is defined as a cost–benefit analysis. There are a number of methods available for measuring outcomes in monetary form, including examining what people actually pay to avoid risks, or, conversely, the premium they will accept to take risks.

Another method is to ask individuals or groups to take part in experiments to value different outcomes in a 'willingness-to-pay' study. Clearly, such studies must be carefully designed to ensure the reliability and validity of the outcome measures. Putting a monetary value on life is problematic at the best of times, and could reflect socio-economic inequities if based on an individual's willingness or ability to pay. This can partly be avoided by using a representative sample of the population in the study.

Identifying, measuring and valuing the costs and benefits of drug prevention

The actual costs and benefits included in an economic evaluation will depend on the questions asked and the perspective taken.

Costs of drug prevention

The costs of prevention activities fall into four main groups:

- direct costs to the agency delivering the intervention;
- direct costs to other agencies involved in the intervention;
- direct costs to the individuals participating in the intervention; and
- indirect productivity costs.

The direct costs of the intervention include all staff costs and resources (such as leaflets, telephone bills, and so on). Many of these costs may be directly observable, although calculating staff time when staff are engaged in more than one intervention may present some difficulty. It is important, however, to include all resources used – including capital and management expenses – in the intervention. The proportion of fixed costs, such as buildings or equipment, and semi-fixed costs, such as staff, help to determine the ratio between total direct costs and the proportion of the intervention delivered. Some programmes, for instance, may incur considerable initial capital costs. If only a few participants are attracted, the average cost per participant would be extremely high. The marginal cost, or cost for every extra person, would then fall as the number recruited increased.

Drug-prevention programmes may involve many agencies, especially in community-based initiatives. Support may be given 'in kind', such as volunteer time and donated resources, rather than in the form of directly accounted resources. Such help is often difficult to quantify, but if these resources have a possible alternative use, then they have some form of economic value which should be included in the economic evaluation.

There may also be costs incurred by the individuals involved or their families. Programmes may require travel or other monetary expenses, such as visits to a doctor, while families may need to buy certain items themselves as part of the intervention.

Indirect costs in terms of 'lost productivity' are the subject of some controversy. Clearly, if people undergo treatment or take part in a prevention programme, they are spending time that could be spent on other activities. This lost productivity is usually valued in terms of the individual's earning capacity, and has dominated the results of some health-care evaluations. A way of dealing with this is to present results with and without these indirect costs and benefits (Drummond and Jefferson, 1996).

Benefits of drug prevention

The list of potential benefits of drug-prevention programmes can also be divided into a number of different groups (Rosen and Lindholm, 1992):

* health benefits to the individuals targeted by the intervention;
* consumption benefits of the intervention;
* other non-health benefits;
* social diffusion effects; and
* effects on future resource use.

Which individual health outcome is chosen to be measured will be determined by the economic evaluation design. In a cost-effectiveness study, for instance, only one indicator would be used. In cost-utility studies, health-related quality-of-life measures only cover a limited number of dimensions. Problems associated with drug use, however, include a far wider range of issues, among them physical health, mental health, employment, criminal activity and personal relationships. Prevention programmes could have an effect both on an individual's quality and quantity of life across one or more of these different dimensions.

It could, therefore, be argued that some of the many existing measures are inadequate to capture the full range of effects. Perhaps some super-QALY is needed that would include more than health dimensions, for example, some of the life skills, self-esteem and other consumption benefits that form part of many primary-prevention drug programmes. Alternatively, some means of capturing these different effects in terms of willingness to pay or other monetary measure could be viable. However, the danger of choosing one effectiveness measure over another is that other outcomes may not be perfectly correlated with the chosen measure and could lead to an incorrect comparison between the programmes.

Drug-prevention programmes can also provide a range of potential social benefits. Rosen and Lindholm (1992) suggest that the outcomes of many interventions are underestimated because effects are measured only on the participating individuals. They argue that additional benefits arising from the social diffusion of the intervention throughout the community must be recognised. Such effects can be seen, for instance, in the large reduction in smoking in many European countries.

Society may also benefit from a low rate of drug-related problems as a result of a successful prevention programme. These may be in the form of direct effects, such as a lower rate of HIV infection, or in the form of reduced resources needed for health, social-care and criminal-justice activities directed at drug misusers. In the case of drug treatment, these social benefits from reduced drug use have been substantial (see, for example, Gerstein *et al.*, 1994).

Most of these wider benefits are measured in monetary terms. However, not all societies value these benefits equally. For example, in some countries more weight may be given to preventing any drug use than to preventing problems among existing drug users (Godfrey and Sutton, 1996). These values are often reflected, if not made explicit, in current policy decisions. Therefore, when undertaking an economic evaluation, the value system used to measure individual and social benefits has to be made explicit.

Steps required in planning an economic evaluation

Planning an economic evaluation involves a number of major steps. Several texts give more detailed step-by-step guidance for undertaking such studies (Tolley, 1992; Drummond *et al.*, 1997; Gold *et al.*, 1996), but this chapter will consider the following issues:

* defining the study's economic issues and perspective;
* choosing the alternatives to be evaluated;
* designing the study to collect both benefit and cost data; and
* planning the data analysis, including discounting, sensitivity analysis and incremental measurement.

The perspective and purpose of the study, as discussed above, will help decide which preventive interventions to compare. The choice of which alternative interventions to evaluate is obviously a crucial part of any study. Comparing two prevention initiatives and finding one to be more cost-effective than the other is not much help to providers or policy-makers if a third promising option was not included in the study. The narrower the question being addressed the easier it becomes to trace all possible options, including the status quo approach. Including a status quo option is important in this early stage of knowledge about the cost-effectiveness of drug prevention. Any new initiative should, therefore, be compared to any current one.

It is clear that no programme can be judged 'cost-effective' if it is not also 'effective'. The design of the study to determine both costs and benefits needs to be robust. Reviews of the evaluation of workplace testing programmes have highlighted some of these specific issues. Many studies have suggested that pre-employment drug screening benefits employers. Dinardo (1994) suggests, however, that because most designs have been observational rather than experimental in approach, it is difficult to attribute causality. Drug users differ from non-users in many ways, and hence the observed work differences between those testing positively for drugs and those who do not may just reflect these differences in characteristics and possible confounding effects. These and other broader study-design issues are covered in other chapters.

Ideally, economic evaluations would take place alongside other forms of evaluation. One alternative is to use effectiveness evidence from reviews and to compile the resource and cost data either retrospectively or prospectively. In prevention programmes, many of the benefits may occur in the future and it would be difficult and costly to observe these effects. Epidemiological models may therefore be used with the review or observed-effect data. Holtgrave and Kelly (1996) provide an example in which the effects of HIV prevention programmes from a trial were modelled to identify gains in QALYs, while the cost data were calculated using data from the same trial. Likewise, Kahn (1996) examined HIV prevention using epidemiological models and reviews of effectiveness data to simulate the number of HIV infections avoided by increasing the budget by $1 million.

These are clear examples of the fact that the costs and benefits attached to different prevention programmes often manifest in different time periods. In general, benefits are sought immediately while the costs are delayed for as long as possible. Obviously, prevention programmes follow the reverse pattern, with costs incurred at the outset while some (if not all) of the benefits become apparent only well into the future. In order to make some comparison, therefore, it is necessary to put the costs on some common, usually current, value system. In most commercial activities, costs and benefits that occur in the future are given a lower weight.

Consider a prevention programme aimed at reducing deaths from overdose. For sim-plicity's sake, this is assumed to result in ten people each living five years longer from the year the programme was conducted. Undiscounted, this is a total of 50 life years. Discounting at 5% yields 10.0 years in the first year, 9.5 years the second year, 9.0 years the third year, 8.6 years in the fourth year and 8.2 years in the fifth year – an estimated total of 45.3 life years gained from the prevention programme.

Discounting health benefits will lower the comparative cost-effectiveness of preven-tion programmes. Parsonage and Neuburger (1992) have set out the arguments for and against such discounting, and conclude that studies should report a range of discount rates on benefits, including the undiscounted figures. As well as life years gained, discounting will also affect projected future savings on health, criminal-justice and other welfare services, although there is more consensus that non-health benefits should be discounted. Discounting may also alter the results of a cost-effectiveness analysis within population groups, possibly favouring older groups or those with existing drug habits who may benefit in the short rather than the long term.

Economic-evaluation techniques provide a framework, but all studies require a number of assumptions to be made at every step of the process. Some costs and benefits may be omitted, and assumptions may be made about the size or variability of effects or resource use. Clearly, the sensitivity of any results to changes in these assumptions must be tested in some way.

Conclusions and the use of study results

Economic evaluations can have powerful results, proving that one type of inter-vention is not as cost-effective as another. However, the general lack of cost-effectiveness information can cause the results to be over-generalised from one specific evaluation to a more general situation. This over-generalisation can, of course, create all sorts of problems.

Such problems can partly be avoided by adopting good practice as outlined in general economic texts. The major problem, however, is the lack of evidence. The paucity of existing research means that many studies must have larger research components if some of the complex issues raised in this chapter are to be tackled effectively. The lack of economic evaluation also means that individual studies cannot cross-check their findings against others. This creates the danger of stretching a study beyond its design to answer the wide-ranging questions to which policy-makers want the answers. The obvious solution is to undertake more economic evaluations, but this involves resources and prioritisation. Even with a paucity of data, there is still a considerable advantage in undertaking preliminary work, so that the most important economic questions can at least be established.

Economic evaluation has been seen as a necessary, but sometimes unwelcome, addition to other types of evaluation. The challenge now is to make economic evaluation more accessible, and to demonstrate its use as a tool for making more explicit policy choices and illuminating the value system by which such decisions are made. It is clear that this form of evaluation must be based on robust study designs as discussed elsewhere in this monograph, but there is also a need to develop adequate economic measures relevant to drug-prevention programmes.

Acknowledgements

This chapter draws in part on a review of the costs and benefits of drug programmes in the workplace undertaken by the authors for the UK Health Education Authority, although the views expressed in this chapter are the authors' own. The authors are also grateful to Dr Gerhard Bühringer and Dr Enrico Tempesta who provided very useful comments on an earlier draft.

References

Dinardo, J. (1994) 'A critical review of the estimates of the costs of alcohol and drug use', in MacDonald, S., and Roman, P. (Eds) *Research Advances in Alcohol and Drug Problems,* Vol. II, *Drug Testing in the Workplace,* New York: Plenum Press.

Drummond, M., and Jefferson, T. (1996) 'Guidelines for authors and peer reviewers of economic submissions to the BMJ', *British Medical Journal*, 313(7052), 275–283.

Drummond, M., *et al.* (1997) *Methods for the Economic Evaluation of Health Care Programmes*, 2nd edition, Oxford: Oxford Medical Publications.

Fiscella, M., and Franks, P. (1996) 'Cost-effectiveness of the Transdermal Nicotine Patch as an adjunct to physicians' smoking cessation counselling', *Journal of the American Medical Association,* 275, 1247–1251.

Gerstein, D., *et al.* (1994) *Evaluation Recovery Services: The California Drug and Alcohol Treatment Assessment (CALDATA)*, Sacramento, CA: California Department of Alcohol and Drug Programs.

Godfrey, C., and Sutton, M. (1996) 'Costs and benefits of treating drug problems', in Lunt, N., and Coyle, D. (Eds) *Welfare and Policy: Research Agenda and Issues*, London: Taylor and Francis.

Gold, M., *et al.* (Eds) (1996) *Cost-effectiveness in Health and Medicine*, New York: Oxford University Press.

Holtgrave, D., and Kelly, J. (1996) 'Preventing HIV/AIDS among high-risk urban women: the cost-effectiveness of a behavioral group intervention', *American Journal of Public Health*, 86(10), 1442–1445.

Kahn, J. (1996) 'The cost-effectiveness of HIV prevention targeting: how much more bang for the buck?', *American Journal of Public Health*, 86(12), 1709–1712.

Parsonage, M., and Neuburger, H. (1992) 'Discounting and health benefits', *Health Economics*, 1(1), 71–76.

Rosen, M., and Lindholm, L. (1992) 'The neglected effects of lifestyle interventions in cost-effectiveness analysis', *Health Promotion International*, 7(3), 163–169.

Rydell, C., and Everingham, S. (1994) Controlling Cocaine: *Supply Versus Demand Programs*, Santa Monica, CA: RAND.

Shipley, R., *et al.* (1995) 'Community stop-smoking contests in the COMMIT trial: relationship of participation to costs', *Preventive Medicine*, 24(3), 286–292.

Single, E., *et al.* (1996) *International Guidelines for Estimating the Costs of Substance Abuse*, Ottawa: Canadian Centre on Substance Abuse.

Tolley, K. (1992) *Health Promotion: How to Measure Cost-effectiveness*, London: Health Education Authority.

CHAPTER 9

EPIDEMIOLOGY, PREVENTION AND EVALUATION

Richard Hartnoll

The first priority of the EMCDDA, as specified in its founding Regulation, concerns the demand for drugs and reducing that demand. In operational terms, this is reflected in the Centre's organisation and in the creation of the two departments that deal primarily with the scientific content of its work programmes: Epidemiology; and Demand-Reduction. The relationship and relevance of epidemiological information and research to the implementation and evaluation of demand-reduction activities is thus a central issue.

This chapter examines selected examples of areas in which epidemiology can be of practical value to drug prevention and prevention-evaluation research. It begins by briefly examining what epidemiology is and how it relates to drug prevention and evaluation research. The chapter concludes with suggestions for areas in which co-operation would increase the synergy between epidemiology and prevention research, and for mechanisms that might encourage greater cross-fertilisation, to the mutual benefit of all involved.

Epidemiology, prevention and prevention research

Epidemiology is sometimes perceived as an esoteric science for collecting and analysing statistics, and one that is distinct from prevention interventions and evaluation research. In fact, this is misleading and misrepresents the purposes and functions of epidemiology, even if the misperception is an understandable one. Epidemiology is concerned with questions that are fundamental if policies and interventions are to be based on evidence rather than on preconception and to develop in a relevant and effective manner. Wherever an epidemiological approach is applied – be it in the field of infectious diseases with which it is traditionally associated, or in areas such as smoking and lung cancer, environmental pollution and asthma, or drug use and drug-related problems – it addresses common key issues. These issues include:

- identifying and describing the nature and extent of a problem or phenomenon (its prevalence, distribution in the population, characteristics and consequences);
- investigating the 'how' and 'why' (aetiology, risk and protective factors, mechanisms and processes);
- examining the design and evaluation of interventions (for example, random controlled trials or community interventions); and

* epidemiological surveillance of trends and identification of new problems (monitoring and early-warning systems).

An important additional component in the drugs field, although not unique to this area, has received greater emphasis than in other, more traditional areas of epidemiological research. This is the application of qualitative ethnographic, sociological and behavioural research methods to complement statistical investigations. The reason for this, in part at least, is that drug use and drug addiction are complex phenomena with cultural, social, historical, economic and psychological as well as pharmacological dimensions. Furthermore, individual and collective subjective perceptions play an important role in shaping the behaviour and responses of all involved, whether drug users or non-users, the general public, practitioners, researchers or policy-makers. Statistical data and analysis can provide the structured and 'objective' framework necessary for describing and monitoring the phenomenon, for testing hypotheses about its aetiology, and for designing and evaluating interventions. However, this is often insufficient for interpreting the patterns and trends that are observed within their local or national context, or for appreciating the all-important nuances of how the different actors perceive, construct and react to the world as they understand it. This takes on even greater significance when comparing across countries and cultures. Broadening the epidemiological paradigm thus adds to the potential for linking epidemiological data to the development of policies and interventions.

Why, then,.the perception of some practitioners that epidemiology is not really relevant to their daily work? A comparison with the emergence of epidemiology in the field of public health is illuminating. Historically, epidemiology developed within the context of public-health practice as a practical tool to help identify and monitor problems, and to design and evaluate interventions. There was thus no real gap, either between epidemiology and public-health interventions, or between epidemiology and evaluation research. Public-health practitioners have been, and usually are, also epidemiologists.

Epidemiology in the drug field developed relatively autonomously as a research-oriented discipline dealing with questions that often tend to be more relevant to policy-makers than to practitioners. As noted above, epidemiology expanded beyond the original medical model to incorporate many elements from disciplines such as sociology, anthropology, social psychology, psychiatry and economics. However, many interventions in the drug field, and especially prevention, have grown out of other sectors, for example social services, counselling, education or health promotion. It is not surprising, therefore, that a gap exists between practitioners and epidemiologists. They come from different backgrounds and have different training. Most practitioners (in prevention at least) are not involved in research, and researchers are rarely involved in prevention.

Furthermore, prevention research has often involved social scientists who do not consider themselves to be epidemiologists, even though many of the techniques they use are similar to those used in epidemiology and many of the methodological issues with which they are concerned – for example, study design, sampling, control groups or inferring causality – are identical. Prevention and epidemiology are not really separate disciplines and have much more in common than is sometimes recognised.

Relevance of epidemiology to prevention

Three examples demonstrate how epidemiological data and methods can be of relevance to drug prevention and evaluation:

* *Drug problems and needs assessment* Is there a problem and if so what sort of problem is it and what are the needs? How far do existing interventions and prevention efforts address them? What are the dimensions and characteristics of the target groups most at risk?
* *Early identification of emerging trends* How to identify important new trends and potential problems in time to develop appropriate preventive measures.
* *Evaluating the impact of drug prevention* Do interventions reach their targets? What is their impact at individual level? What is their impact at group or community level?

Drug problems and needs assessment

One of the first questions that epidemiology addresses is 'how many?' – how many drug users? How many addicts? – or, in other words, prevalence. The answers are usually sought either through surveys of the general population or of subgroups, such as school pupils, or through estimates based on various registers or indirect indicators, for example of people treated for drug problems or those arrested by the police. Some non-epidemiologists may consider this as the major goal of epidemiology. However, for the purposes of developing responses and interventions, a simple prevalence figure begs more questions than it answers. This can be illustrated by the fairly narrow example of assessing needs in relation to problems related to opiates, in particular heroin. Issues regarding the broader spectrum of drug use, drug problems and prevention will be discussed later in this chapter.

For example, a prevalence study may conclude that there are around 100,000 heroin addicts in a given country. But so what? Is this a large number, or only a few? Is the number increasing or not? What are the characteristics of the individuals involved and of the communities most affected? What sorts of problems and costs are implied by such a figure? What are the major needs, what types of interventions are most appropriate, and how should resources be allocated?

In this hypothetical yet realistic scenario, the value of an epidemiological approach lies not in the figure itself, but rather in following up the questions that such a figure raises. To take the first question – is this a large number of addicts or not? – the initial step is to set the number against the size of the population of the country concerned. In the smallest EU country, Luxembourg, this would represent 25% of the whole population, a level of heroin addiction probably unmatched in any society in history. In the largest country, Germany, it would represent a little over one-tenth of 1%. In practice, the range in Europe is towards the lower of these two extremes, and is typically under 1% of the total population. So the question remains: is this a serious problem or not, and if so, in what way is it serious?

Continuing for the moment to focus on the example of heroin addiction, even if its prevalence represents a small proportion of the total population across a whole country, the distribution of that prevalence can be, and often is, very uneven. Heroin addiction in many European countries at present occurs primarily in the 18–40-year-old age range, especially amongst males, and can be associated with various cultural, social and individual risk factors. It can also be highly concentrated in cities or in certain districts within major metropolitan areas, for example amongst more socially marginalised or disadvantaged communities with high unemployment rates and other social problems, and in some cases in areas linked to heroin trafficking and distribution. This means that prevalence can be many times higher than the national average, for example up to 5–10% among young people in the highest-risk groups or communities.

A thorough epidemiological analysis would go beyond a detailed description of how the prevalence is distributed in the population to examine its health and social consequences. These can include the demand for treatment for drug-related problems, such as addiction, the level of excess mortality and the extent of other drug-related health problems, such as infectious diseases or non-fatal overdoses. Investigations of the social consequences are less commonly included in epidemiological assessments, and can in any case prompt a debate about the boundaries of epidemiology. Issues here can include drug-related crime, the extent to which addicts and other drug users are arrested or are imprisoned, or the characteristics and possible dimensions of illicit drug supplies and drug markets.

What is the value of this sort of information? On the one hand, information about addiction, its prevalence, distribution and characteristics can be very relevant to the provision of treatment services. For example, are there enough treatment centres, are they situated in the right places, do they offer services that are appropriate to the characteristics of the addicted population and important subgroups within it? Information on hidden populations who are not well provided for can be particularly useful, since treatment staff tend to identify needs in terms of the problems presented by the clients whom they do see rather than those they do not. The information may also be useful for developing harm-reduction programmes (for example, on changing patterns of drug injection or on factors such as risk perceptions and others associated with sharing needles). More broadly, information on the scale and nature of drug problems and associated needs – as well as their implications in terms of costs – provide valuable ammunition for arguing for adequate resources to target well-identified problems.

On the other hand, this information refers to a phenomenon for which prevention, by definition, is already too late. What, then, are the implications for prevention? It would be a mistake to see epidemiological information on prevalence, problems and needs related to heroin addiction as irrelevant to prevention or early interventions just because the data immediately to hand refers to already addicted groups. Valuable lessons can be learned from these and other historical data, both in terms of the risk factors that they identify, and in terms of the light they cast on the processes by which heroin use and addiction become established and spread within communities or develop over time in individuals.

Information on the risk factors of problematic patterns of drug use – such as heroin addiction – or of serious consequences – such as overdose or HIV infection – is rather scattered across the literature. One of the tasks on which the EMCDDA has recently embarked is to review and synthesise some of this information, taking account of other useful reviews that have already been undertaken. It is clear, however, that the notion of risk factor should be extended beyond individual or family characteristics to the environment, including the socio-economic dimension and situations linked to problematic drug use or risky behaviour. It is also necessary to include what could be called 'developmental epidemiology', which seeks to integrate individual developmental patterns with environmental and contextual processes. Although no single blueprint for prevention is likely to emerge, this body of knowledge should give a more informed basis for identifying interventions that offer greater possibilities for slowing rather than increasing the development of problematic drug use and its adverse health and social consequences.

Regarding the processes by which heroin use and addiction spread and become established within communities, an accumulating body of epidemiological evidence, for example from the United States and some European countries, suggests a degree of consistency in the longer-term patterns and cycles of so-called 'heroin epidemics'. It is important to avoid simplistic generalisations on this point, both because there are important local variations, and because significant innovations can arise that alter some of the parameters of these epidemiological models – for example, new routes of administration (such as heroin smoking), new risks (such as HIV infection) or new combinations of drugs (such as crack cocaine). However, despite these reservations, some broad and common themes have emerged, both across countries and over time.

Models for analysing these patterns are still at a relatively early stage of development. However, even without a detailed analysis, it is realistic to suggest that in the long term, in higher prevalence areas where heroin use and addiction are established and endemic, prevalence is likely to continue at broadly similar levels for the foreseeable future, despite short-term fluctuations in the incidence of new cases and changes in the age distribution of the addicted population. If so, then the prevalence figures suggested earlier would translate on average into at least one – and possibly up to three – potential heroin addicts in every school classroom in a high-risk area. If the example is broadened beyond heroin addiction to include other heavy and problematic patterns of substance use, then the challenge for prevention should be clear. A further example of the long-term evolution of patterns in drug use and drug problems is that 'epidemics' in larger cities often spread some time later to smaller towns and rural areas, a pattern that can be seen in some European countries. Thus it is important to anticipate needs by, for example, training professionals or developing models of service delivery that are appropriate to larger, low-density areas.

An under-developed level of analysis, but one that is receiving increasing attention, concerns not only the consequences of drug addiction, but also the social and economic costs that these entail. As in the case of prevalence, the consequences and their costs are likely to be much more substantial in some areas or on some topics than in others. Here, too, the process of differentiation renders the information much more valuable than the sort of global figure with which this analysis began. This allows priorities and targets to be set that correspond more closely to actual needs than to preconceived notions of the nature of the problem.

Apart from prevalence, consequences and costs, a comprehensive assessment of problems and needs can address the lifestyles of drug users and the social contexts of their drug use. Alternatively, it can address their experiences and perceptions of risks, prevention messages and treatment services. This can give insight into the social, economic and cultural constraints that have to be taken into account when implementing strategies and interventions. Such a project could examine public knowledge, attitudes and perceptions about, for example, fears related to drug addiction, or attitudes towards prevention and treatment that could help in developing information strategies and interventions that will gain acceptance.

Information of the type described in this example is of considerably greater value for developing effective and informed interventions than the simple prevalence figure with which this section began. A similar exercise could be undertaken starting with the results of a school survey, taking the finding, for example, that '20% of 15-year-olds have tried cannabis at least once in their lives'. This would engender a similar process of step-by-step delineation and elaboration of questions. The result would be the same – that it is not the prevalence figure itself that is the important contribution of epidemiology, but rather the answers to the questions that lie behind that figure.

Early identification of emerging trends

The previous section examined the assessment of problems and needs related to established and more problematic patterns of drug use, such as heroin addiction. This section examines some of the issues involved in identifying new trends or anticipating emerging problems in time to take appropriate preventive measures.

The starting point for this discussion is a 'prevention dilemma'. If there is no problem, prevention is either not needed or, if it is, what must be prevented? If, however, there is a problem, prevention is needed, but it is already too late.

Many countries undertake prevention activities based on the assumption that some form of pre-emptive prevention is needed, and on the (valid) observation that drugs are available and used to a greater or lesser extent in virtually every community across the globe. These activities tend to be broad, fairly non-specific programmes aimed at discouraging drug use in general or at providing information about the effects and risks of different drugs in the hope that this will have a preventive effect by promoting informed choices. Other approaches are set within broader perspectives that do not specifically single out drugs, such as health education and healthy lifestyles. Some might also argue that other social programmes can have non-specific drug-prevention effects, for example programmes concerned with crime prevention, reducing social exclusion, promoting urban renewal or stimulating community involvement.

The priority and level of resources devoted to drug prevention in this general, pre-emptive sense often seems to reflect the level of social and political concern more than it does the objective level of drug use or drug-related problems. However, in cases where public and political pressure reacts to increases in identified, more specific patterns of drug use or drug problems by demanding more prevention, then the second part of the dilemma becomes apparent: it is already too late. Yet, the response might then be that it is not too late for subsequent generations. In part, this may be true, but it makes the questionable assumption that approaches developed with reference to the problems of yesterday's generation are appropriate to the as-yet-to-be-observed problems of tomorrow. How relevant were the preventive messages aimed at discouraging heroin use or the sharing of syringes in the 1980s to the increased use of synthetic drugs in the 1990s?

The dilemma becomes important once the discussion moves from the general, non-specific level to the question of how to identify, track and understand new trends to distinguish whether and in what ways they are potentially serious, and to do so in a timely fashion. The demand is thus for information that enables intelligent and appropriate responses to be implemented quickly, but which does not generate false alarms or lead to preventive actions that are misinformed and lacking in credibility. This highlights the need for reliable early-warning indicators that identify emerging trends and problems in time for more focused and appropriate actions to be taken if necessary.

This prevention dilemma raises a parallel one for epidemiology. Indicators reflect changes in drug use and drug-related problems only after they have already occurred. If the goal is to identify new trends before they have emerged, then how to measure what does not yet exist? And when it does emerge, how to know that a trend is a trend until after it has indeed become one? Even the less ambitious goal of improving the ability to track trends and identify problems at an earlier stage than is currently the case presents a serious challenge.

New trends in drug use, like many innovative developments, usually first arise in specific localities or in restricted social groups or settings. Methods such as surveys of the general population or of school pupils cannot identify these trends until some time after the behaviours have been more widely adopted, nor can reliable measurements be obtained until the prevalence has risen to quantifiable levels. Traditional indicators based on problematic consequences, such as the demand for treatment or other health issues, are also slow to respond, since in many cases there is a time lag between, for example, first use and first contact with a treatment centre (if indeed there is any contact).

There are several ways of developing methods for identifying, tracking and understanding new trends. Most of these are based on networks of key informants. These key informants include people in touch with groups where new trends in drug use are most likely to be observed at an early stage. While the list may vary between countries and local contexts, it could include researchers (especially qualitative researchers carrying out fieldwork amongst different groups of drug users), local practitioners in the fields of prevention and harm reduction (especially those involved with user groups, outreach activities and at-risk groups of young people), and a diverse collection of others (for example, workers in the youth media and entertainment industry).

A complementary approach could be to use forecasting models to project trends, based not only on epidemiological models of drug use, but also on sociological and market-based models of the diffusion of innovation and fashion. This could include monitoring music and other youth-cultural magazines, Internet sites and similar forms of communication.

The feasibility of improving epidemiological monitoring to identify new trends more rapidly and reliably is currently being studied by the Epidemiology Department at the EMCDDA. The Department is examining the possibilities described above, and more concrete results should be available by the end of 1998. Two key aspects are how to assess the reliability of reported trends, and how to understand their significance.

In parallel with improving epidemiological systems for monitoring new trends, it is essential to establish links with practitioners in the field of prevention and harm reduction so that the information can be applied in a relevant manner. This implies that those practitioners who are in the best position to apply the information should also be involved in the network of key informants who provide the information in the first place. One way to link epidemiology and prevention in this field is to build the partnership into the system from the beginning. This linking is probably best pursued at local level, which is where the data originates and where the results will be implemented.

Evaluating the impact of drug prevention

The other chapters in this monograph deal with different aspects of evaluating drug prevention. This section is thus restricted to selected critical observations that an epidemiological perspective can provide – although, as noted earlier, there is an important degree of overlap between epidemiology and prevention research.

Epidemiological methods can provide information relevant to the evaluation of several questions: do preventive interventions reach their targets? What is the outcome of prevention? What is the impact at individual level? What is the impact at group or population level?

An appropriately designed epidemiological study can describe the knowledge, attitudes and perceptions of the population, the distribution of drug use and the characteristics of the users within that population, and analyse some of the risk or protective factors associated with drug use or non-use. Since many prevention activities are school-based and targeted at school-aged children, this population is used here for illustrative purposes.

The most common method for studying drug use in school populations is an anonymous, self-completion questionnaire given out in the classroom. A large number of such surveys have been carried out in Europe and elsewhere. Sometimes they are conducted primarily for research purposes to measure levels of drug use in that population and/or to study risk factors, and the results may only indirectly feed into prevention measures. In other cases, they are carried out as part of a prevention programme so as to identify levels of experience, knowledge and attitudes towards drugs and, on occasion, also to evaluate changes that may be linked to preventive interventions.

Other methods for studying this age range include household surveys that sometimes involve those as young as 12 – although such surveys more commonly start at age 16 or 18 – and a variety of more targeted studies of selected groups of young people, including those in a range of non-school settings.

The results of these surveys and other studies suggest that large differences exist in experiences of drugs, not only between countries or localities, but also between school-age children with different characteristics. Sometimes, these characteristics are described as risk or protective factors, although whether they are risk factors in a causal sense is unclear. It is likely that many would be better described simply as correlates of broader dimensions that characterise adolescents and their lives. Certain common themes emerge from all these studies, although there is also an important degree of divergence in terms of the presence and relative importance of so-called risk and protective factors.

The strongest and most consistent theme is that experience of drugs increases very quickly between the ages of 12 or 13 and 19. This refers both to the proportion who try illegal drugs (which can increase from a small percentage at age 12 to over 30–40% or more by the ages of 18 or 19) and to the number of different drugs they take. This is presumably why drug prevention is targeted at schoolchildren (although this is also a fundamental period of personal development and transition in a much broader sense). The rapid increase in drug use over this period is also a major obstacle to evaluating prevention, since there appears to be a built-in bias towards failure. How to plan evaluative studies to overcome this problem is beyond the scope of this chapter, but involves at a minimum carefully selecting control groups within a longitudinal design.

A second consequence for evaluating prevention in the steep gradient observed in drug use between the ages of 12 and 20 is related to the diversification of school careers after the age of 15 or so. In many countries, some young people stay in academic schooling, whilst others move to a variety of vocational or technical schools. In other countries, a significant proportion leave school to begin work (or not), and others, in anticipation of leaving school, do not attend so frequently. This means that a diminishing proportion of young people aged 16–19 are still in the school system where they received their drug education, and in many cases they are no longer in settings covered by school surveys (many school surveys do not involve the older age range). The significance of this for evaluating prevention increases if the transition from schoolchild to young adult and from school to vocational training, work or unemployment is itself an important risk (or protective) factor for drug use or for increased consumption of a wider range of drugs.

In this respect, data on the age of first use of different drugs based on school-survey data, for example among 15-year-olds, excludes by definition any initiation after that age and can give a very misleading picture of the ages of first use and patterns of initiation in the population as a whole. This is especially true of drugs other than cannabis. For example, in many countries, the most common age for initiation into heroin or cocaine (amongst people who subsequently enter treatment) is around 19 or 20 or sometimes even older.

This presents serious problems in evaluating whether the drug prevention has any longer-lasting impact on behaviour, either on an individual or on an aggregate basis. Thus, most evaluation studies of changes in individuals rely on short-term or proxy measures, such as knowledge and changes in attitude, perceptions of risk or the expressed willingness to try drugs. Unless the evaluation design is longitudinal and longer term, there is no way of knowing whether any relationship exists between school-based prevention and various other factors, behaviours or attitudes measured before the age of 16, and behaviour thereafter. Assuming that those who remain in the school system are representative of those who do not begs the question of whether or not school-based prevention has a protective effect on subsequent non-school behaviour. Nor does it take any account of whether leaving school is itself a risk (or a protective) factor and if so under what circumstances. The same limitations hold for evaluations based on measures of drug use in school surveys of young people above the ages of 15 or 16.

A further issue with implications for evaluating school-based prevention is whether evaluations measure separately the impact of prevention on the highest-risk groups, who by definition are most in need of prevention (although see the prevention dilemma referred to above – it may already be too late), or whether global measures are used that refer to the school population as a whole (or at least to those who received the prevention). It is quite conceivable that prevention messages have least effect, or even a negative effect, on those at highest risk, but their main impact is to reinforce the non-drug attitudes of those at lower risk. The balance of the effects will probably depend on whether the school concerned is in a high- or low-prevalence setting, a factor that may also influence the nature of the risk factors identified. A special case involves how to influence truants, who are likely to constitute a particularly high-risk group, but who are also likely to be absent both from drug-prevention sessions and from school surveys that measure their behaviour.

There is no doubt that attempting to evaluate the impact of prevention is a formidable task. The methodology required to analyse these complex issues is probably beyond the resources of most evaluation designs. The corollary is that considerable caution should be exercised when reporting the results of any evaluation of school-based prevention, especially when the data both on drug use and for evaluating prevention are collected solely from those at school.

Conclusions: linking epidemiology, prevention and prevention research

In conclusion, epidemiological analysis offers powerful tools for examining a simple prevalence figure to tease out some of the complexity of the phenomenon, to identify risk factors, risk groups and risk situations related to drug use, the development of addiction and its consequences, to assess the relative costs of those consequences, and to differentiate problems and processes that in turn imply differentiated responses. Epidemiological analysis can contribute to the identification of emerging trends and to the evaluation of interventions. It can also, although this has not been considered here, offer models of drug use and drug problems relevant to developing a theoretical framework to underpin prevention strategies, for example the question of whether prevention should aim to reduce the level of drug use in the population as a whole, or whether it should simply focus on high-risk groups.

It must be added, however, that this potential has often not been fully exploited and even less commonly have the results been communicated in intelligible or useful fashion to those who could use them. It should also be noted that information and analysis of data at the national or European level provides a framework, but that most value for practice is likely to be achieved at the local level through collaboration between local policy-makers, researchers and practitioners. The potential may be substantial, but so too is the task of realising that potential.

This chapter has also touched on how closer links could be established between epidemiology and prevention, between research and practice. On a pragmatic level, the way forward is to build in these links from the very beginning of any prevention project – that is, to design interventions as multi-disciplinary efforts involving both practitioners and researchers (including epidemiological researchers where relevant). Conversely, relevant epidemiological studies should involve practitioners from an early stage as both information providers and information users.

At another level, epidemiologists and researchers are responsible for making greater efforts to render their information both intelligible to practitioners and accessible to them in a way that they can use. Conversely, it is the responsibility of prevention practitioners, especially perhaps those who hated mathematics at school, to accept that practice is based on theory, whether implicit or explicit, and that both theory and practice can be analysed constructively and evaluated using both quantitative and qualitative evidence and methods. This involves more than just producing and exchanging attractive and well-written booklets. It should also include face-to-face encounters and joint projects where some of the mutual wariness of each other's roles and some of the barriers to communication can be resolved. This may be easier to say than to do, but this is true of all partnerships.

CONFERENCE WORKSHOPS

INTRODUCTION

*T*he six workshops summarised here all took place at the 'First European Conference on the Evaluation of Drug Prevention', held in Lisbon in March 1997. Further workshops discussed the draft of the EMCDDA's Guidelines for the Evaluation of Drug Prevention, *but, as 'work in progress', these are not reported on below.*

The first workshop covered mass-media public-information campaigns and how they can be used in the field of drug prevention. They were categorised in two ways: as a monologue; and by the fact that many 'speakers' were involved in attracting the attention of the target group. The workshop developed a model of a mass-media campaign with four stages, ranging from initial contact with the message to its final acceptance. The group felt that such communication could usefully complement traditional one-to-one prevention techniques, although it was crucial to evaluate them adequately.

The second workshop discussed how prevention interventions can be constructed to deal with synthetic drugs and their users. Because the use of ecstasy was such a recent development, few interventions – many of which had been set up almost overnight with little planning – had been fully evaluated. This local level of sponta- neous prevention had also at times been reflected at the regional level, where find- ings from earlier evaluations were not taken into account. Preventing synthetic drug use, therefore, requires a strong base of evidential research, and young people's expectations of the form and content of preventive messages should be analysed on an almost daily basis. Standard prevention techniques that stress controlling con- sumption tend to be rejected by synthetic drug users, who generally view their drug use as a 'lifestyle choice'. Furthermore, synthetic drug use often takes place in social situations, while prevention is conventionally undertaken on a one-to-one basis. The workshop concluded that, for these reasons, prevention strategies for this particular target group need to focus on harm reduction rather than on primary prevention.

The third workshop examined the issue of prevention and its evaluation in the com- munity setting. It was quickly established that to avoid resistance to the programme and doubts about its outcome, all those who could be affected by an intervention should be involved in its implementation and evaluation. Programme-planners should always be prepared to encounter problems when designing a community strategy, as issues of participation, responsibility and transparency are never far from the surface. This means that drawing up a timetable is essential, as is recognising the often delicate balance of power that may exist between individual players. Compromise is therefore the key to successful community working. The group also discussed any 'value-added' objectives and agendas that different participants may pursue in evaluating the intervention.

The fourth workshop tackled youth culture. It was felt that cultural influences were too often ignored when planning prevention activities, creating a shortfall between the amount of time spent on the 'message' and the time spent on its intended 'audience'. The problem is that those prevention activities that do define their target groups in terms of lifestyle are normally difficult to evaluate. The workshop therefore felt that more research needed to be carried out if a consideration of 'youth culture' was to be incorporated into basic prevention interventions, and to enable prevention measures to be more subtly differentiated.

School-based prevention was the subject of the fifth workshop, which discussed the issue as a natural, continuing part of the curriculum. It was accepted that since this form of prevention should progress from non-specific primary prevention to more targeted secondary prevention, it was very difficult to refer to any generic target group, as different age groups had different needs. While the workshop felt that schools were appropriate settings for educational prevention strategies, how to develop those activities was open to debate. The relative involvement of teachers and parents in a prevention intervention was discussed, and it was generally agreed that it was difficult to convince teachers of the need for 'global prevention' in schools, while parents are rarely involved in developing prevention strategies. Since evaluation relates to the whole development process, it was agreed that a realistic outcome measurement needed to be discussed in advance.

The sixth workshop looked at peer-led prevention. If young people are to heed a prevention initiative, it must be credible in their eyes, and peer-based programmes may be the best way of ensuring this. As part primary prevention, part harm reduction, such schemes are, however, resource-intensive. The controversy surrounding peer education was mirrored in the group's discussions, with disagreement as to whether drug users should be used as peer leaders and whether abstinent peers can deliver effective harm-reduction messages. Some group members felt that peer-led prevention helped increase knowledge, but had little effect on behavioural change. Others, however, saw sharing knowledge as a peripheral component of peer-group prevention.

WORKSHOPS

Mass-media campaigns

Chaired by Jürgen Töppich

In his introductory presentation, Jürgen Töppich explained the characteristics of mass-media communication before examining the process model of persuasive messages. This model is linked to the planning and evaluation stages of prevention initiatives, and can be used to evaluate current mass-media campaigns.

Two essential features characterise mass-media communication: first, it involves a one-way communication from a 'sender' to an anonymous 'recipient'; and second, many senders vie for the attention of the target audience.

According to the process model, mass-media communication involves four main stages:

* the recipient is physically contacted and exposed to the communication;
* the recipient becomes aware of the message;
* the recipient understands the message; and
* the recipient accepts and absorbs it.

Ways of planning and evaluating mass-media campaigns can be derived from these four stages. During planning, a major consideration is how to expose the recipient to the message. This involves selecting appropriate media and channels of communication, as well as assessing the frequency and intensity of exposure to the message. In order to hold the recipient's attention at the second stage, the message must be attractive and appealing. Linguistic style and mode of expression, the scope of the message, and the quantity and depth of the information it contains are therefore highly relevant at the planning stage. The logic and clarity of the argument, its credibility and any educational elements must also be included in the planning process if the message is ultimately to be accepted by the recipient.

Exposure to the message during the first stage must be evaluated, while attentiveness during the second stage can be assessed using recall tests, depending on the length of contact with and interest in the message. This may still not be enough, however, to verify whether the message has been fully understood (the third stage). To verify this, the recipient must be able to reproduce the content and substance. As a final stage, the degree to which the message has been accepted must be evaluated by any changes in or confirmation of intentions.

In the discussion that followed Töppich's introduction, it emerged that one of the problems identified with mass-media campaigns was that social groups other than the target group may respond to the message and so confuse the evaluation. Preliminary tests should thus be carried out to prevent unwanted reactions.

In order to reach the target group, appropriate media must be selected. Radio was considered a tried and tested means of reaching young people, while the target group itself could help to evaluate the campaign by participating in a listener phone-in.

It was also seen as more difficult to define and assess the intended effects of a mass-media campaign than when using face-to-face communication as measures, since campaigns are frequently intended to encourage or support change.

Evaluating what would happen if no campaign was run was seen as good practice, and the only way to ensure that the assumed effects of a campaign were not measured by time alone. The group considered a number of ways to approach this evaluation problem. One solution was to compare the expected development (with no campaign) with the actual development (with a campaign). Another was to compare two regions or countries (one with and one without a mass-media campaign).

As well as highlighting the problems of evaluation, specific mass-media campaigns were provided as examples. One of these, the 'stark statt süchtig' ('better strong than addicted') campaign from Vorarlberg, Austria, was judged to have successfully combined mass-media campaigns with face-to-face prevention.

In sum, mass-media campaigns were seen as important tools that could usefully complement face-to-face prevention. However, verifying the effectiveness, and therefore evaluating, a campaign was also considered vitally important.

Ecstasy and other synthetic drugs

Chaired by Roger Lewis and Jim Sherval

By way of introduction, Roger Lewis and Jim Sherval discussed their involvement in an EMCDDA project to review ecstasy-related interventions in Europe and their evaluation.[1] Lewis and Sherval also provided a brief definition of the term 'synthetic drugs': psychoactive substances artificially produced in laboratories from chemical raw materials (precursors) rather than from natural products. In this instance, the term refers to ecstasy and its analogues, amphetamines and LSD.

In the subsequent discussion, it was asked whether preventive measures should be geared towards events associated with the drug scene, or whether they should be more broadly based. A number of participants felt that the media indirectly encouraged the use of synthetic drugs, as young people often do not believe what is reported about drugs. The irrational, knee-jerk reaction of many politicians to the ecstasy phenomenon was also criticised.

Because ecstasy had spread unpredictably and rapidly, low-level projects had been established relatively spontaneously without built-in evaluation. Many programmes had yet to be evaluated at a higher level. Sometimes, badly planned and poorly

---

[1] This project formed the basis for part of the EMCDDA's publication, *New Trends in Synthetic Drugs in the European Union* (Insights Series, No. 1).

designed measures had been implemented at the regional level, without taking sufficient account of findings from earlier preventive and evaluative research. Often, no primary-prevention measures had been taken in the early stages of the ecstasy phenomenon because the emerging use of synthetic drugs seemed not only to be containable within an integrated society, but also socially less conspicuous than, for example, heroin use. Although some medical advice had been given, this had not been evaluated either.

Evidence of the ecstasy phenomenon was beginning to emerge in areas that had previously experienced no problems. While the use of this type of drug had now become the subject of primary prevention, little still seemed to be known about ecstasy users. Several studies have revealed that ecstasy users are not in fact a completely new target group, but are also usually cannabis users. Ecstasy users had been involved in developing earlier initiatives, and one view was that preventing ecstasy use, compared to other substances, posed no specific problem. What was new, however, was that ecstasy was seen as fun and enjoyable by its consumers and often not as a 'drug' at all.

How youth culture could be influenced was also discussed. Despite differences between countries, the ecstasy culture has acquired a degree of uniformity in much of Europe through music, radio, video and other events. Effective prevention, therefore, requires researchers to analyse young people's expectations on an almost daily basis – in the same way that promoters of new drug-related styles do – given that these expectations are constantly changing. This ongoing analysis could form part of a strategy of better communication with ecstasy users. They often know when to stop using the drug, a decision generally linked to poor work performance and a loss of enjoyment associated with excessive consumption.

In this context, the group also discussed what messages had been found to provide useful prevention information. Since such messages normally entail controlling consumption, those relating to synthetic drugs were often rejected by the target group. Another dilemma is that consumption often takes place in social situations, whereas prevention tends to occur on an individual basis. For these reasons, strategies should now be geared towards harm reduction rather than primary prevention.

The dynamics of harm reduction and primary prevention were repeatedly discussed. At what point is a certain level of consumption acceptable, if ever? It was agreed that it is important to find out what matters to young people, so that appropriate action can be taken. A shift from primary prevention towards harm reduction was felt to be visible across the spectrum, from high-level politics to on-the-spot measures.

Work in the community

Chaired by Fernando Bertolotto

In his introduction, Fernando Bertolotto stressed the need to involve all concerned in a prevention initiative in its implementation and evaluation. This would help to prevent any resistance to the work or doubts about its outcome. Working in the community also means involving non-experts, something which may alarm the experts. The problems that arise in such situations relate above all to issues of participation, responsibility and transparency.

As a result, some convergence of opinion must be sought amongst all the community players. It is also important to remember that when working in the community, setbacks will occur and the project may at times come to a complete standstill. It is therefore essential to create a timetable. Recognising the balance of power between individual players is likewise vital, and allowances have to be made to ensure the project's success. Thus, when working in the community, compromise is always necessary.

Members of the community will be all too aware that evaluating the work is linked to programme funding. Regardless of the actual outcome, evaluation therefore also depends on the commissioning body's agenda. In the case of drug prevention, a kind of 'social compromise' is often arrived at between funders and implementers. This represents a prior agreement on the general outcomes that cannot be compared to scientifically based results. Evaluation, however, should be seen as a continuing part of the process, not as a retrospective assessment.

In the discussion that followed, it was proposed that working in the community is only possible if the programme's objectives are perfectly clear and do not conflict with the individual's work. Setting prior goals is essential, as most programmes still have no clear objectives in terms of their target groups or outcomes.

Community work is rarely rational and tends to be influenced by emotion. As a result, scientifically objective criteria cannot always be applied. Evaluation has to take full account of this subjectivity, and not merely apply and implement statistical techniques. Neglecting this aspect could have far-reaching implications for future cooperation in that particular community.

Another view was whether evaluation should focus purely on technical issues, such as process, outcome, demand reduction or dependency. Evaluation can be carried out at a conceptual level, taking into account ideological aspects, such as cultural, ethical or moral values.

The difference between the design of a prevention programme and its actual implementation was pointed out. While the programme must have a strong scientific basis, its implementation in the community must be geared to that community's specific problems. Creating and sustaining the motivation to undertake the programme is a highly complex process, but all those involved – be they politicians, the public or the administrative authority – must share that motivation. It is therefore necessary to involve all concerned, because everyone is needed to carry out the project as a whole.

It was also mentioned that, in some circumstances, the various groups involved pursue different objectives to those laid down by the programme. These 'value-added' objectives should also be included in the evaluation.

It was felt that the ultimate objective of community-based initiatives is always difficult to define, since it is impossible to determine in advance whether a reduction in demand or an increase in community safety could be achieved in any other way. It may be easier to evaluate the outcome in a single setting, such as a school or home, but the problem is far more complex in an unbounded community. The community is thus a far-from-ideal setting for evaluation, since it is heterogeneous and subject to constant changes in time and place. Owing to the large number of players and participants involved, change is only possible in the very long term. Regarding organisational development, the only way to achieve change is to pursue a bottom-up strategy rather than a top-down one. However, one- or two-year funding arrangements do not allow for long-term planning, even though it would take 10–15 years to achieve any real change.

Another difficulty this group identified is that prevention programmes are frequently commissioned by people who are not part of the community at all. It is therefore important to involve community members in the process so that they can accept some responsibility for, and not undermine, the work. The same applies to the evaluation. In the community, many unforeseen factors prompt constant change, including changes to the programme. Evaluation in the community, therefore, must always be related to the process as an intermediate variable.

Youth subcultures

Chaired by Alfred Springer

In his opening presentation, Alfred Springer introduced four areas for discussion:

- special features of prevention interventions in the 'youth-culture' setting;
- characteristics of evaluation in this area (for example, special methods of data collection);
- features of process evaluation; and
- the evaluation of results.

Incorporating subcultural lifestyle patterns into everyday culture is perhaps the most fundamental problem when addressing youth culture. The sociocultural level of influence is all too often neglected in planning and developing drug-prevention campaigns. One of the main weaknesses of current prevention work is that the primary interest at stake is the message itself, its content and how it is presented. On the other hand, too little attention is focused on the senders and recipients of that message.

The workshop examined various levels of preventive work within the area of youth culture. Many of these initiatives define their target groups in terms of culture or lifestyles, and are therefore difficult to evaluate. Some non-specific, school-based primary preventions also take youth culture into account. Research into different media should be included in the catalogue of basic prevention-research disciplines, and the drug-related aspect of youth-oriented media must be thoroughly investigated.

At the start of the discussion, the term 'subculture' was abandoned in favour of 'lifestyle', which it was felt could be described with a whole range of associative symbols, such as music, clothing, magazines and so on.

The point was made that as the 'techno/rave' scene was highly differentiated, how should prevention projects approach such a disparate array of target groups? It was proposed that youth culture should be regarded as a 'free space' which should not simply be taken away from the young. The workshop saw drug misuse as an actual stabilising factor in youth culture – it would be an entirely new concept in drug prevention if it were implemented only in places where young people were not at risk. It was further argued that risk-taking was a feature of adolescence and that prevention would therefore have to set standards and impart values. It was emphasised, however, that primary prevention was essential to ensure that drug culture did not completely take over youth culture.

It was agreed that identifying trends was a further problem faced by research in this area. In some cases, too much attention had been focused on developments that were not actually trends (ecstasy use, for example).

Setting up international studies to compare youth cultures was also discussed. It was observed that there are extremely significant differences between national youth cultures, with youth lifestyle playing a greater role in, say, the UK than in Sweden.

Furthermore, it was emphasised that the aim of prevention was to help young people overcome difficulties. An important, hitherto neglected strategy for doing so was to ask young people what they needed in order to cope with the risks. In this way, a basis for both prevention and evaluation could be created.

In conclusion, there was a call for preventive measures to be more subtly differentiated. Previous findings should be used and future measures devised in such a way that statements can be made about specific aspects of prevention among youth cultures.

School involvement

Chaired by Michel Orban

After briefly outlining his experience in the field of primary prevention, Michel Orban discussed how prevention can be undertaken with different age groups. The prevention activity should be seen as an integral part of the school curriculum, progressing from non-specific primary prevention to more targeted secondary prevention. It is therefore impossible to refer to any specific 'target group', since different age groups require different programmes.

The success of a school project largely depends on whether teachers support the idea of a prevention programme. As the people best suited to undertake the work, they are initially the most important intermediate target group. While external health-education staff can also be involved in this process, teachers should deal with it first, since they are involved in the general process of education. Professional experts could in turn train and supervise the teachers to allow the intervention to be extended to the final target group – the pupils.

In general, the group felt that the school was a good place for a comprehensive, educational, prevention strategy. As well as providing straightforward information, this approach includes developing children's psychosocial skills, as prevention should not just be aimed at drug use, but at all deviant behaviour. As people of trust, teachers can also offer guidance in personal development. To date, however, it has proved difficult to convince teachers that 'global prevention' in schools could also correct other forms of deviant behaviour.

A school's demand for a prevention intervention is invariably linked to the urgency of the school's drug problem. At present, however, parents tend not to be involved in the discussions that lead to a call for prevention, and they are seldom mentioned as a target group.

A possible reason for this is that young people do not wish to talk about their problems with adults, especially their parents. The family structure is changing so much that it is becoming increasingly difficult for parents and children to understand one another. Hence the need for mediators who can pass on messages and explain concerns. It was suggested that the pupils themselves should choose these 'mediating people of trust'. However, it must be remembered that many teachers are unable to distance them-selves from their pupils' problems and can thus react rather like parents.

Since parents are not formally involved in the education process, under certain conditions they might oppose the implementation of a prevention programme. Parent involvement was discussed, and although it was favoured, it was felt that in some cases pupils might not want their parents to be involved in their problems.

All the factors that might facilitate or impede the planning, implementation and evaluation of a programme must be considered. It is extremely important to ascertain whether the programme can be incorporated into the normal curriculum and whether it can be co-ordinated with other school projects. Moreover, a positive climate in the school was seen as vital for promoting the programme. Another important, but often overlooked, issue in prevention planning is the institutional arrangements for the programme, such as the size of the class.

School development – changing both the institution as a whole and the individuals within it – is a lengthy process which cannot be accomplished in a few days. Merely introducing a prevention programme is a complex matter, and it is not always possible to give funding bodies any absolute measurement of the programme's effect. The evaluation of school-based prevention activities relates not just to the effects actually achieved, but to the whole process of development. It was accordingly felt that a realistic outcome measurement should be discussed in advance.

Peer-group approaches

Chaired by Michael Shiner

Michael Shiner emphasised that credibility was the most important element in making young people take notice of a prevention programme, and that peer-led initiatives were the most likely form of initiative to succeed. These initiatives should be viewed as part primary prevention, part harm reduction. However, process evaluation has revealed that such an intensive approach is costly in terms of resources, particularly time and support.

The group discussed whether drug users should be used as peer leaders, and the involvement of ex-users was regarded as a problem. They might either directly or indirectly convey the impression that giving up drugs is 'no big deal' and that life could be lived to the full before giving up. The complex interaction between the personality of the peer leader and the message being put across was also recognised. Some of the group felt that harm-reduction messages delivered by abstinent peers was highly questionable.

However, this was countered with reference to psychotherapy research, which has found that abstinent peers can be used to convey primary-prevention messages effectively. It was also felt that attention should be focused on the interests of the target group rather than on the interests of those working towards prevention – people who had no experience of drugs would often have little credibility with the young. However, one participant reported rather negative experiences of using peers as leaders: they were poor listeners and unable to communicate their message effectively. It was therefore preferable for them to support the intervention leaders than to take the lead themselves, particularly during the planning stage.

The issues of selecting and training peers were also raised. One view was that if training was so expensive, it may in fact be cheaper to send the members of the target group who are most at risk on a suitable one-week course. But it was also felt that, if properly planned, costs could be reduced.

Peers should not be defined in terms of use or abstinence, but rather in terms of attitude, dress code and age. The involvement of drug users was not essential. Instead, it was felt that the emphasis should be placed on experiences and personality, not on the pharmaceutical properties of drugs. However, whether a peer leader was for or against drug use was, of course, important.

Why young people would believe a peer was also discussed, as was the position of the peers among their own contemporaries and friends. There were also felt to be ethical problems with requests for teachers not to be present, and a related issue was that the expectations of programme-developers did not always match the actual message which the target group received.

Some members of the group felt that using peers increased knowledge, but did not change attitudes or behaviour. However, another participant reported some success in terms of behaviour – abstainers were often strengthened in their resolve – although no change was evident in the case of socially integrated drug users. As for the content of the programme, some participants felt that knowledge was not an absolutely essential component. But others felt that knowledge could be important, since young people have to contend with much uncertainty and many untruths.

CONFERENCE
ROUNDTABLE

PART IV

INTRODUCTION

*T*he last working session of the 'First European Conference on the Evaluation of Drug Prevention' was introduced by a roundtable discussion entitled 'How to Promote Evaluation Practice in Europe?'.

Michaela Schreiber, from Germany's Federal Ministry of Health, chaired the discussion and introduced the other participants:

- *Wim Buisman*, Manager of International Programmes, Jellinek Consultancy, Amsterdam, and Director of the European Addiction Training Institute, Amsterdam.
- *Armand Wagner*, Luxembourg Ministry of Health, and Member of the EMCDDA Management Board.
- *Véronique Wasbauer*, European Commission, Directorate General V, Brussels.
- *Alan Lopez*, Programme on Substance Abuse, World Health Organisation, Geneva.
- *Enrico Tempesta*, Permanent Observatory on Young People and Alcohol, Rome.

ROUNDTABLE

How can drug professionals interest politicians in evaluation?
How can evaluation help with the daily allocation of funds?
How can policy-makers be supported in their discussions?

Buisman was not optimistic about the benefits of presenting the results of evaluations to politicians. Persuading policy-makers of the importance of drug prevention must take their own position into account, and the media can play a major role in doing so. Emphasising the whole picture, not just focusing on the drug users, is equally important. If 1% of young people in Europe use drugs, then 99% do not, and whether this can be presented as a success or not must be taken into account.

Wagner referred to his daily experience of politicians at the Luxembourg Ministry of Health and understood why drug professionals complain about politicians. This complaint is based on inconsistencies between politicians' public statements and their actions, a lack of understanding of the drug professional's work and a lack of financial support for long-term activities. Drug professionals for their part, however, should also try to 'understand' politicians.

Evaluating drug-prevention activities is of more interest to professionals and the general public than to politicians, as it allows the professional to step back from and reflect on daily practice. However, the differences between politicians at the local, national and European level should not be forgotten, and while budgetary choices reflect political decisions, drug professionals are in a position actively to seek funds. Drug-prevention activities should help develop positive approaches to life and make parents and teachers more aware of the fundamental problem of drugs. Ultimately, the public should be more directly involved.

Wasbauer felt that, above all, the aim of evaluation has to be clearly defined. Evaluation is about more than just justifying funding – it should first of all support the professionals working in the drug-prevention field. It is therefore important to distinguish between qualitative improvements in evaluation and their institutional or political justification. In fact, measuring the costs of non-intervention – as has been done with the European Commission – can bring home to politicians the importance of prevention activities.

Just as politicians need to be told about the impact of measures they have already taken, they need information to help them make decisions about measures to take in the future. They should therefore be informed clearly and concisely about the intermediate and final objectives of prevention.

A core issue in budgetary discussions is the cost-effectiveness of a strategy. The lack of information about this aspect can only be damaging, as, in the final analysis, politicians have to answer to their electorate. As Eurobarometer surveys demonstrate, the electorate is largely in favour of repressive measures. Perhaps drug professionals should try to influence the opinions of the European public?

Lopez agreed that politicians need to know what works, under what conditions and at what cost. Policies and programmes must be founded on good science, and politicians' ability to understand good science should not be underestimated.

Evidence should be clearly presented and unambiguous. Politicians should also know the benchmarks against which prevention evaluation is measured. Equally, policy-makers need to know what does *not* work. For example, prevention activities have often been carried out which have not been shown to have a positive outcome, especially regarding tobacco control.

A culture of positivism needs to be instilled around a combination of different prevention measures ('a prevention cocktail'), which may work better than one measure alone. Such a cocktail may also be politically more acceptable.

Tempesta saw the relationship between policy and drug use as very complex, a complexity which is often encouraged by politicians. In some cases, too many prevention programmes have received significant funds without changing attitudes, and this has left politicians disillusioned. As a result, in Italy at least, the general attitude is to leave drug users well alone.

Policies, however, are now more oriented towards local and regional interventions. The scientific world, therefore, has to elaborate community interventions using research knowledge which can be adapted and evaluated at the local level.

The Chair commented that all those on the panel make political decisions themselves by influencing prevention decisions. The issue seems to be whether global aspects or good evaluative practice is used to influence politicians.

Buisman supported Lopez's approach and Wasbauer's first statement. Does it make sense to provide politicians with evaluation results? Sometimes it seems that even with this knowledge politicians make the wrong decisions – in the Netherlands, the Minister of Health is increasing the budget for mass-media anti-smoking campaigns even though evaluation shows that the last campaign failed.

Reactions from the floor were that the current situation is too confusing for decision-makers. The problem may not be so much one of evaluation, but of the speed with which the drug problem evolves. *David Turner* (International Council on Alcohol and Addictions) felt that there was a danger in speaking of politicians, as all participants are 'politicians' in their own field. Reducing the issue to a discussion between experts and politicians is not enough – the community and target groups should also be involved. Life is not rational, so all involved should be 'politicians', and be modest in their attempts at evaluation. Finally, scientists do not only have to bring new knowledge to decision-makers; decision-makers also have to look for new science.

In conclusion, it was agreed that politicians appear to be motivated – as proved by many political programmes on prevention and evaluation – but they are not sufficiently informed and do not always act on the information they have received.

How can duplication between institutions be avoided?
How can evaluation results be used by practitioners?

Tempesta pointed out that in Italy, centrally directed school programmes have received funding for a long time. Only in the 1990s did financial resources begin to be allocated to regional, local and city governments. This generated a great many initiatives, and the general public became aware of the scale of the drug problem. Thus, facing up to drug misuse has to be seen in the community context – how can experience and local creativity be made more widely available? This context is fundamental, and is also valid at the European level. A programme carried out in three European cities to examine people's attitudes towards alcohol found different views in each city.

Lopez believed that the issue is one of 'operationalising' prevention research. Results need to be communicated scientifically, as there are many prevention outcomes (changes in attitudes, increased personal resources, higher age of initiation into drug use, shortening the careers of drug users). From the public-health point of view, prevention evaluation should focus on behavioural change.

Other organisations such as the World Health Organisation should also be lobbied to help instil a culture of monitoring. Institutions are often asked about what works, but it is difficult to find actual evaluation results. The Programme on Substance Abuse, for instance, attempts to instil a culture of monitoring and evaluation in every project it supports, and it favours approaches that involve both project-funders and project-operators. By involving them from the start, any fears felt by the operators can be addressed.

Buisman pointed out that before discussing the need to avoid duplication and improve co-ordination, what it was that needed to be co-ordinated should be identified.

There should first be more consensus on the theoretical base, while not forgetting that although programme development has been greatly emphasised, programme implementation has received little attention, and without implementation there is no evaluation.

Furthermore, no long-term or follow-up studies are being carried out in Europe. Concentrating on behavioural change is a challenge, but it is also problematic. Practitioners and researchers should therefore co-operate more.

Trying to avoid duplication and enforcing co-operation is precisely one of the tasks of the EMCDDA, and the European Commission and other funding bodies can also avoid duplicating their efforts. One possible co-operative venture could actually result from this Conference itself – the establishment of a European Society of Drug Prevention made up of the Conference participants.

Wagner agreed that more co-ordination is necessary, especially at the European Commission level, where a dozen Directorates General are involved in drug issues. In general, the European prevention sector could be much more effective if it adopted long-term approaches and coherent evaluation.

Reactions from the floor were that evaluation is a very heterogeneous concept which has to be clearly defined – for instance, behavioural-oriented efficacy studies are very different from quality control in a small programme. The current state of knowledge of prevention and evaluative research is very difficult to assess. Perhaps the EMCDDA should attempt to do so with a public, peer-reviewed competition to gain an overview of past and present actions.

In conclusion, the need for increased co-operation and the flow of reliable information between researchers, practitioners and international organisations was generally recognised. Suggestions for improved co-operation included focusing on behavioural change, theoretical consensus and monitoring evaluation.

What is the EMCDDA's role in this field?
Are the first steps taken by the EMCDDA with the publication
of the *Guidelines for the Evaluation of Drug Prevention* important,
and should they be continued?

Wasbauer said that the EMCDDA's mandate is to collect and disseminate information about evaluation and its results in Europe, including transnational evaluation projects financed by the European Community's prevention programme. This is a long-term process and the current *Guidelines for the Evaluation of Drug Prevention* and this Conference are just one aspect of it. They should be applicable to different settings and practices, and answer the question of how drug professionals can be convinced of the need for evaluation.

Lopez saw the Conference as a very valuable first step. Establishing common guidelines makes sense, as normative standards are needed, just as in other fields. The EMCDDA should have a 'clearing-house' function, acting as a repository for information and promoting training in evaluating prevention. The Centre can also help countries to get the science right, advise on what outcomes to measure and help to define the appropriate conceptual framework for evaluation. Essentially, the EMCDDA can play a critical role as a catalyst in forging intellectual partnerships, investing in epidemiological methods and promoting the view that prevention research is part of the epidemiological continuum.

Tempesta believed that the EMCDDA should be the production centre for the spread of a culture of prevention through the National Focal Points. The *Guidelines* should be translated into each country's language so that all actors can familiarise themselves with the evaluation concept.

Wagner was satisfied that the EMCDDA was playing an active role in diffusing information on evaluation approaches in Europe. Progressively reliable data are being transmitted at the European level, but a problem remains in that the EMCDDA's mandate only mentions illicit drugs, whereas most prevention activities deal with dependence diseases.

Conclusion

In conclusion, it was agreed that the EMCDDA has a key role to play in collecting and disseminating information about evaluation and its results in Europe. As such, it should act as a catalyst for promoting partnerships, training and good practice.

CONCLUSIONS

CONCLUSIONS

This monograph has traced the history and general characteristics of drug-prevention evaluation, as well as its technical and practical elements. It has given some major examples of evaluation research, as well as information about the methods and instruments used. In addition, the workshop reports illustrate the use to which the EMCDDA *Guidelines for the Evaluation of Drug Prevention* can be put in the most common settings for drug prevention – schools, mass media, youth groups, the community and peer groups – and regarding synthetic drugs. The summary of the roundtable held at the end of the Conference highlights the major issues raised in the discussion on how to promote evaluation in Europe. Some important conclusions can be drawn from this work and from the Conference itself.

Evaluation is necessary

The level of accurate evaluation in Europe is still low. Yet current knowledge about prevention and how it works has only been gained through thorough evaluation studies. As large-scale preventive activities are implemented more and more in Europe, it is becoming increasingly necessary to evaluate them. Owing to this close link between prevention practice and research into drugs, evaluation within a programme structure should be an integral part of daily work, not a specialist task. Scientific advances must be communicated to practitioners in a way that they understand and are able to use. While prevention research has made good progress in developing and testing new models for family, school and community-based programmes, evaluation studies are still required to validate these programmes and to test various ways of putting them into practice.

Barriers have to be overcome

Among the barriers that need to be overcome are the fear of negative or unexpected results. These fears, however, should be seen rather as challenges and cornerstones for further improving programmes, since identifying a programme's weaknesses is just as important as identifying its strengths.

The central challenge for drug professionals is to convince politicians of the need for evaluation, and the European Union can play a key role in this. Its institutions can become a forum in which to agree a set of evaluation standards. This monograph itself, and the accompanying *Guidelines for the Evaluation of Drug Prevention*, are successful examples of the European effort to promote such a strategy. Co-operating with research institutes and universities, as well as co-ordinating various programmes, can reduce the costs of investing in evaluation.

Evaluation is more than just assessing the outcomes of interventions

Outcome evaluation (results) is important, but process evaluation (the 'how' and 'why' certain results are obtained) is even more so. The need to strike a balance between the two has been underlined in this monograph, since outcome cannot be interpreted effectively without sound information on processes. Process evaluation is necessary for improving prevention and providing feedback to those involved.

Evaluation must be thoroughly planned

In any evaluation, it is essential to involve all the actors from the planning stage to the dissemination of the results, as transparency is a key issue at all stages. This is especially true for community prevention programmes. Since different actors have different agendas, defining goals and processes involves constant negotiation. In cases where an evaluation has not been planned and agreed by all the evaluators, the process will be disturbed. From the beginning, evaluation calls for public relations and communication skills: as evaluation is a tool to improve and develop future preventive work, it is essential that people accept it and pay attention to its recommendations.

Evaluation helps to structure preventive strategies and to enhance their impact

Every prevention programme has a theoretical background, if only in the mind of the programme-planner. Experts in the field have demonstrated that, if these theories are sound, they may not only provide a framework for understanding health behaviour, but also help to define the outcome of drug-prevention efforts. In turn, if implemented properly, these efforts may increase knowledge, enhance social norms and attitudes opposed to drug use, increase social skills and eventually decrease drug consumption.

A need to develop methods

Purely experimental designs for scientific evaluation have proved to be inadequate in practice and do not provide sufficient information on policy-relevant issues. Instead, qualitative and quantitative methods should be combined, provided that the results can be generalised and their validity ensured. Prevention programmes based on theoretical models that involve analysing mediating variables help in interpreting outcomes and improving the intervention.

Evaluation instruments required

Standardised evaluation instruments are essential, and the reliability and validity of these tools is the key to sound results. Reliable instruments do exist, but evaluators need to use them properly. The contributors noted that evaluation instruments are often invented for, and geared to, specific studies, which makes comparison across projects difficult. Special instruments for process evaluation are important, because assessing the quality of a programme's implementation is highly relevant for its success.

The role of epidemiology

Developing a partnership between epidemiology and prevention is another key requirement. It is acknowledged that the science of epidemiology provides instruments for evaluation and for measuring outcomes, and can also help prevention experts to define problems, needs, objectives and target groups. However, epidemiological indicators cannot always keep pace with the needs of prevention experts, who are often called upon to respond to situations urgently. In this context, the challenge for epidemiologists is to identify new trends and problems in a way that enables prevention experts to respond rapidly.

Economic considerations

Economic evaluation has been seen as a necessary, but sometimes unwelcome, addition to other forms of evaluation. Estimating the costs and benefits of interventions in monetary terms is difficult, and efforts should continue to help calculate the value of outcomes. In all countries, the resources available for drug prevention are limited and both programme-providers and funders are keen to get value for money. However, the success or failure of a prevention may only become apparent many years later, and it is therefore very difficult to measure in economic terms.

The major problem in this area is the lack of a body of evidence, but even with the little data that exist, ongoing preliminary work should be undertaken so that major economic issues can at least be established. Economic evaluation must be made more accessible and its advantages as a tool for making more explicit policy choices demonstrated. Adequate economic measures suitable for drug-prevention programmes must therefore be developed.

Practical aspects of evaluating special preventive approaches

Mass-media preventions

Evaluating mass-media prevention should focus on how the recipient is exposed to the message (its frequency and intensity), its attractiveness and appeal, as well as on the recipients' attentiveness and interest in the message. To verify whether it has been understood, the content and substance must be reproduced by the target group. Finally, whether or not the message has been accepted must be evaluated through any changes or confirmation of intentions.

Community interventions

In evaluating community interventions, scientifically objective criteria are not always applicable since much of the work in a community is affected by subjective factors and is rarely rational. This makes it more difficult simply to apply and implement scientific methodology and statistical techniques. Implementing a prevention programme in a community should be geared to the specific situation of that community. In evaluating community interventions, it is essential that features such as cultural, ethical or moral values are assessed.

Youth culture

In evaluating prevention in the context of youth culture, it is important to ask young people what they feel they need to help them cope with the risks they perceive in their daily life, since the aim of prevention is to help young people overcome difficulties.

CONTRIBUTORS

Dr Gerhard Bühringer
Institut für Therapieforschung (IFT)
Parzivalstrasse 25
80804 Munich
Germany
Tel: (+49) 89 36 08 04 60
Fax: (+49) 89 36 08 04 69

Jutta Künzel
Institut für Therapieforschung (IFT)
Parzivalstrasse 25
80804 Munich
Germany
Tel: (+49) 89 36 08 04 60
Fax: (+49) 89 36 08 04 69

Dr Zili Sloboda
Director
Division of Epidemiology and Prevention Research
National Institute on Drug Abuse (NIDA)
5600 Fishers Lane 9 A5 3
Rockville
MD 20857
USA
Tel: (+1) 301 443 6504
Fax: (+1) 301 443 2636

Teresa Salvador-Llivina
Director
Centro de Estudios sobre Promoción de la Salud (CEPS)
c/ Carretera de Humera 60
28224 Pozuelo de Alarcón
Madrid
Spain
Tel: (+34) 1 351 53 61
Fax: (+34) 1 351 53 37

Dr Christoph Kröger
Institut für Therapieforschung (IFT)
Parzivalstrasse 25
80804 Munich
Germany
Tel: (+49) 89 36 08 04 80
Fax: (+49) 89 36 08 04 59

Thomas Jertfelt
Consultant
Nordöstra Sjukvordsomrodet Bestallarstaben
Plan 9
18287 Danderyd
Sweden
Tel: (+46) 8 655 7410
Fax: (+46) 8 622 5890

Han Kuipers
Trimbos Institute
Netherlands Institute for Alcohol and Drugs (NIAD)
PO Box 725
3500 AS Utrecht
Netherlands
Tel: (+31) 30 297 1125
Fax: (+31) 30 297 1128

Mark Morgan
St Patrick's College
Drumcondra
Dublin 9
Ireland
Tel.: (+353) 1 837 6191
Fax: (+353) 1 837 6197

Christine Godfrey
University of York
Centre for Health Economics
York Y01 5DD
UK
Tel: (+44) 1904 433718
Fax: (+44) 1904 433644

Steve Parrott
University of York
Centre for Health Economics
York Y01 5DD
UK
Tel: (+44) 1904 433718
Fax: (+44) 1904 433644

Jürgen Töppich
Bundeszentrale für gesundheitliche Aufklërung (BzgA)
Ostmerheimer Str. 200

51109 Cologne
Germany
Tel: (+49) 221 899 2342
Fax: (+49) 221 899 2300

Dr Roger Lewis
Centre for HIV/AIDS and Drug Studies (CHADS)
Lothian Health
148 Pleasance
Edinburgh EH8 9RS
UK
Tel: (+44) 131 536 9371
Fax: (+44) 131 536 9376

Jim Sherval
Centre for HIV/AIDS and Drug Studies (CHADS)
Lothian Health
148 Pleasance
Edinburgh EH8 9RS
UK
Tel: (+44) 131 536 9374
Fax: (+44) 131 536 9376

Fernando Bertolotto
Consultant
9 Mas des Pérols
34470 Pérols
France
Tel/Fax: (+33) 467 17 02 03

Prof. Dr Alfred Springer
Ludwig Boltzmann Institut für Suchtforschung
Mackgasse 7a
1237 Vienna
Austria
Tel: (+43) 1 88 82 53 31 12
Fax: (+43) 1 88 82 53 31 38

Michel Orban
Centre d'enseignement et de recherche en education pour la santé (CERES)
Université de Liège BAT C1
Rue Armand Stevart 2
4000 Liège
Belgium
Tel: (+32) 4 252 5859
Fax: (+32) 4 254 1899

Michael Shiner
Policy Studies Institute
100 Park Village East
London NW1 3SA
UK
Tel: (+44) 171 468 0468
Fax: (+44) 171 388 0914

Michaela Schreiber
Bundesministerium für Gesundheit
Am Probsthof 78a
53121 Bonn
Germany
Tel: (+49) 228 941 3260
Fax: (+49) 228 941 4937

Dr Wim Buisman
Jellinek Consultancy
Stadhouderskade 125
1074 AV Amsterdam
Netherlands
Tel: (+31) 20 675 2041
Fax: (+31) 20 676 4591

Armand Wagner
Service d'Action socio-thérapeutique
Ministère de la Santé
1 rue du Plébiscite
2341 Luxembourg
Tel: (+352) 40 47 40
Fax: (+352) 40 47 05

Véronique Wasbauer
EC Commission Directorate-General V
Bâtiment J. Monnet
Plateau du Kirchberg
Office Eufo 3164A
2920 Luxembourg
Tel: (+352) 43 01 32 838 /35 010
Fax: (+352) 43 01 34 511

Dr Alan Lopez
World Health Organisation
Programme on Substance Abuse
Avénue Appia

1211 Geneva
Switzerland
Tel: (+41) 22 791 21 11
Fax: (+41) 22 791 48 51

Prof. Enrico Tempesta
Osservatorio Permanente sui Giovani e l'Alcool
Via Savoia 29
00198 Rome
Italy
Tel: (+39) 6 841 9150
Fax: (+39) 6 841 7383 /305 3949

PRACTICAL INFORMATION

Address:
The European Monitoring Centre for Drugs and Drug Addiction
Rua da Cruz de Santa Apolónia 23–25
P-1100 Lisbon, Portugal

Telephone:
351 1 - 811 30 00

Fax:
351 1 - 813 17 11

E-mail:
General: info@emcdda.org or emcdda@reitox.net
Private: firstname.surname@emcdda.org or firstname.surname@reitox.net

Printed in Italy

EMCDDA, June 1998

European Monitoring Centre for Drugs and Drug Addiction

Luxembourg: Office for Official Publications of the European Communities

1998 - pp. 144 - 16 x 24 cm

ISBN 92-9168-050-8

Price (excluding VAT) in Luxembourg: ECU 17.50